madonnastyle

madonnastyle

by Carol Clerk

OMNIBUS PRESS

London/New York/Paris/Sydney/Copenhagen/Madrid/Tokyo

Contents

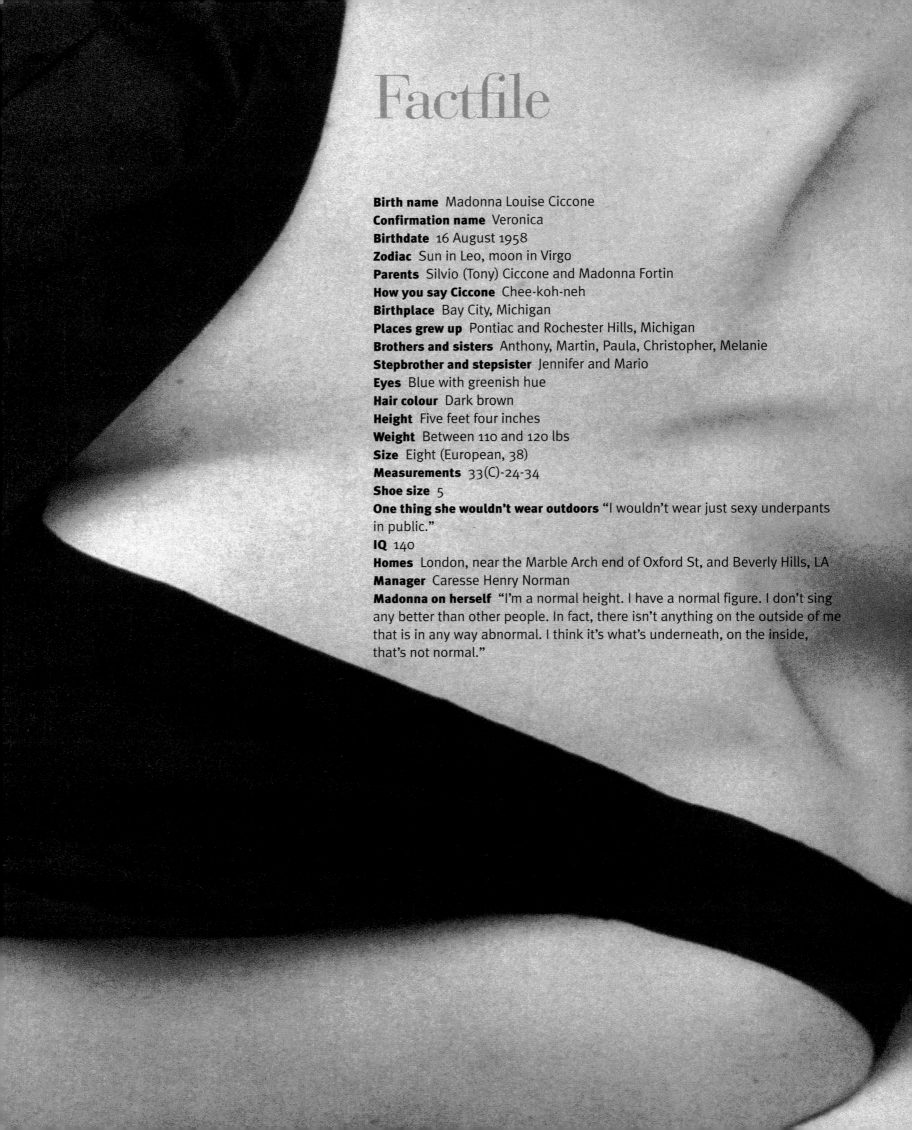

Factfile

Birth name Madonna Louise Ciccone
Confirmation name Veronica
Birthdate 16 August 1958
Zodiac Sun in Leo, moon in Virgo
Parents Silvio (Tony) Ciccone and Madonna Fortin
How you say Ciccone Chee-koh-neh
Birthplace Bay City, Michigan
Places grew up Pontiac and Rochester Hills, Michigan
Brothers and sisters Anthony, Martin, Paula, Christopher, Melanie
Stepbrother and stepsister Jennifer and Mario
Eyes Blue with greenish hue
Hair colour Dark brown
Height Five feet four inches
Weight Between 110 and 120 lbs
Size Eight (European, 38)
Measurements 33(C)-24-34
Shoe size 5
One thing she wouldn't wear outdoors "I wouldn't wear just sexy underpants in public."
IQ 140
Homes London, near the Marble Arch end of Oxford St, and Beverly Hills, LA
Manager Caresse Henry Norman
Madonna on herself "I'm a normal height. I have a normal figure. I don't sing any better than other people. In fact, there isn't anything on the outside of me that is in any way abnormal. I think it's what's underneath, on the inside, that's not normal."

Copyright © 2002 Omnibus Press
(A Division of Music Sales Limited)

Cover & Book designed by
Chloë Alexander
Picture research by
Nikki Lloyd & Carol Clerk

ISBN: 0.7119.8874.9
Order No: OP 48488

Exclusive Distributors
Music Sales Limited,
8/9 Frith Street,
London W1D 3JB, UK.

Music Sales Corporation,
257 Park Avenue South,
New York, NY 10010, USA.

Macmillan Distribution Services,
53 Park West Drive,
Derrimut, Vic 3030,
Australia.

To the Music Trade only:
Music Sales Limited,
8/9 Frith Street,
London W1D 3JB, UK.

Printed in Singapore

A catalogue record for this book is
available from the British Library.

www.omnibuspress.com

Picture Credits

Every effort has been made to trace the copyright holders of the photographs
in this book but one or two were unreachable.
We would be grateful if the photographers concerned would contact us.

Front cover: PA Photos/EPA; back cover: PA Photos/ABACA
AA/Redferns: 69br,87tl
Richie Aaron/Redferns: 28
All Action: 71r,85,88,123,125cr,127tc,139l,157l,159,161,169,170b,172l
Chris Ashford/Camera Press: 145br
John Bellissimo/Retna: 35
Big Pictures: 29t,166c&r
Camera Press: 87bl,127br,150
Capital Pictures: 126bl&r,132,134c,154l
Courtesy Polly Gordon: 124
DK Images: 162,163,164,165
Courtesy Chris Finch: 68,69l
Courtesy Angie Hung: 131
Courtesy Emma Johnston: 130t
Kobal Collection: 52tr, 54inset
L.A.Times/Retna: 143
Gary Lewis/Camera Press: 47r, 142
Michel Linssen/Redferns: 91
LFI:2,5t&b,10,12,13,14,15,19r,24,26,29c&br,32,33,34,38tl&br,39br,40,42,43,44,46
r,47l,50,54r,56,57,60,66b,77r,78l&br,79,86,87br,103,104r,105,110,
111,118,125bl&r,126tc,133,135bl,136r,137,138,147,149,154t,174,175
Ian McKell/Retna: 20
Courtesy Penny McKinley: 130b
Tom Morillo/Keller/Camera Press: 22,23,25
Courtesy Toby Morse: 98t
New Eyes/Redferns: 37
PA Photos: 9,52br,168t&br,173
Pictorial Press: 6/7,19l,54l,55,63,64,65,66t,76,115,125tl&cr,126tr,127lt&b,144
Popperfoto: 107t,108tr,128,160
Neal Preston/Corbis: 96,97,119,122,125
Relay Photos: 5c,58,61,120
Rex: 8,16,31,38bl&tr,39t&bl,48,49b,51,62,69t,70,71l,74,77b,78tr,80,81,82,
83l,87tr,89,92,93,94/95,100,101,102,104l,106,107b,108t&c,109,113,
116,117,121,125tr&cl,126tl&bc,127tr&cb,129,134t,135t&c,136l&c,
139r,140,145t,c&bl,148,151,152,153,154br,155,156,157r,158,166l,167,
168bl,170tl&r,171,172r,176
Ebet Roberts/Redferns: 45,72,73,75
Ronald Grant Archive: 52lt&b,53rt&b
D.Sillitoe/Camera Press: 134b
Sothebys: 46l
Kelly A.Swift/Retna:4
Jurgen Vollmer/Redferns: 67
Jerry Watson/Camera Press: 53tl
Courtesy Mike Watt: 98b,99
T.Wood/Camera Press: 108b

Acknowledgements

With big thanks to Scott Mackenzie for research, Diana Perkins for help
and frontline support, Emma Johnston for her Madonna collection,
Kristy Barker for her thoughtfulness, James Blandford for expert knowledge,
Chris Charlesworth for the opportunity, Stephanie Jones for the "diversionary
reading" and, last but definitely not least, Nigel and Eve O'Brien for their love,
understanding and encouragement.

Bibliography

Madonna: An Intimate Biography by J Randy Taraborrelli
(Sidgwick & Jackson)
Madonna: Blonde Ambition by Mark Bego (Plexus)
Madonna: The Style Book by Debbi Voller (Omnibus Press)
I Dream Of Madonna: Women's Dreams Of The Goddess Of Pop
compiled by Kay Turner (Thames And Hudson)
Madonna In Her Own Words compiled by Mick St Michael (Omnibus Press)
Sexing The Groove: Popular Music And Gender edited by Sheila Whiteley
(Routledge)
Frock Rock: Women Performing Popular Music by Mavis Bayton (Oxford)

Introduction

She was the first female artiste to bring real "girl power" to the mainstream, and she brought it magnificently.

Blazing a trail across the world, vowing from the outset that "I'm in charge of my fantasies... I'm in charge of my career and my life," Madonna has set examples and challenged convention as surely as she has captivated audiences with her contemporary blends of dance and pop.

A genuine superstar in a class of her own, Madonna has revolutionised the world of entertainment with her ability to be all things to all people in her ongoing crusades as the "mother of reinvention".

That she has transcended the traditional boundaries of sex, age and culture so triumphantly is due in no small part to her inimitable personal style.

Madonna – singer, dancer, performer, actress, musician, writer, whatever – is a Jack of all trades and mistress of them all, but she is many times greater than the sum of her parts. That's to do with the way in which she has combined, presented and risen above her talents, and her "way" is truly extraordinary.

Madonnastyle looks in detail at her development as a visual performer in every aspect of her art and her real life, following as she moves from the riotous, street-punk explosions of her early appearance through her controversial mix of erotic and religious imagery, her pioneering use of video and the internet, to the colourful and sophisticated productions that are her forte today.

The changing public faces of Madonna have arisen directly from her personal life experiences. *Madonnastyle* explores a childhood and adolescence that are at the heart of her most memorable creations, charting her struggles with Catholicism, her sexual history and her idealisation of motherhood.

But style is not just about fashion. It's about identity, attitude, personality and lifestyle, and *Madonnastyle* studies, from their origins, the qualities and choices that are an inseparable part of her legend.

Madonna has become an essential role model, a towering example of female potential. The rags of her early career have given way to untold riches, a happy and respectable family life, a fabulous career that she controls herself, and an undiminished influence that can make a worldwide fashion sensation out of a simple T-shirt.

1: THE ROOTS **1958–1985**

"When I was tiny, my grandmother used to beg me not to go with boys, to love Jesus and to be a good girl. I grew up with two images of women: the virgin and the whore."

Good girl, bad girl, virgin, whore... such simplistic characterisations may stand at the outer edges of Madonna's wide and complex spread of imagery, but they are symbolic of a childhood coloured by extremes.

Any one situation might produce a hostile response from the rebellious youngster, while another might be met with an unexpected acquiescence or agreement. Others could well provoke dual and opposite reactions.

The circumstances of Madonna's childhood and the unpredictable and often contradictory personality at play even then have echoed through her work down the years. Combined with her later interest in distorting the accepted, the sacred and the nondescript, they have enriched and given life and depth to her roleplay.

It's also clear that various key events and influences in her formative years equipped the ambitious young dancer with many of the qualities she needed to take on the world and win.

feminine sort of way could get me a lot of things, and I milked it for everything I could," she confessed in an interview in 1989. "I was always very precocious as a child, extremely flirtatious."

Her brother Christopher confirms that Nonnie, as she was affectionately known, did indeed become their parents' favourite, forming a particularly loving relationship with her mother, and was something of a "spoilt kid". She was "really aggressive and wanted her way, and got it," he recalls. "But she was good-hearted. She liked to take care of the bunch. She was also very bossy."

Little Nonnie was soon learning from other cultures. While she was infuriated at being unable to copy the intricate hairstyles of the black girls she befriended, she homed in on the soul music they listened to on their radios and record players, reluctantly leaving them dancing to Motown in the gardens, into the evening, while she returned home to her duties.

Tony Ciccone headed the household with an emphasis on education and discipline, instilling in Madonna a work ethic

"*I grew up with* two images *of* women: the *Virgin* and the whore"

Madonna Louise Ciccone came into the world on 16 August 1958 in Bay City, Michigan, where the family was visiting at the time. The Ciccone family lived in Detroit where Italian descended father Silvio (Tony) worked as a Chrysler engineer. He and his French-Canadian wife, Madonna Fortin Ciccone, already had two sons, Anthony and Martin, when Madonna came along. She was followed in quick succession by Paula, Christopher and Melanie.

By the time she could walk and talk, Madonna had decided to be her parents' star child. She wanted more than her share of their attention, competed for it, and often succeeded. As an adult, she would do the same thing again – although for a considerably larger audience.

Madonna would sing and dance on the table-top like her heroine Shirley Temple, taking care to improvise a show-stopping flash of knicker. She would hurt herself deliberately, for sympathy. She would do something naughty, simply to be singled out for punishment. She would tell tales on her brothers. She would be noisy. But her favourite tactic was more manipulative: she would flirt, and she would flirt again, baby eyes looking out from under a mop of dark, unruly hair.

"I just knew that being a girl and being charming in a

and single-mindedness that remain crucial to her incredible success – no matter how much she may have disliked her father's rules at the time. "If my father hadn't been strict I wouldn't be who I am today," Madonna once conceded.

In this devoutly religious family, regular church attendance was a must, and Madonna's early exposure to Catholicism has left lasting – and conflicting – impressions, many of which she has explored, controversially, in her songs and videos, amid accusations of blasphemy.

As a small child, the awestruck Madonna embraced the passions and the problems of Christianity whole-heartedly and in the most basic terms, visualising herself being tugged this way and that by God and Satan. Only later would she begin to question and reject the oppressive and destructive aspects of a faith that, in other ways, still attracts her.

"I do believe religion and eroticism are absolutely related," she explained to writer Norman Mailer in August 1994. "And I think my original feelings of sexuality and eroticism originated in going to church... it's very sensual, and it's all about what you're not supposed to do. Everything's forbidden, and everything's behind heavy stuff – the confessional, heavy green drapes and stained-glass windows,

Madonna has always been inspired by the glamour of Hollywood, reincarnating the spirit of Monroe in shots like this, snapped in 1987 by Herb Ritts and used for the Who's That Girl tour poster.

Madonna was raised in a strict Catholic atmosphere, and outfits like those worn for her confirmation (above) may explain her later penchant for wedding dresses. By the age of 19 the star was already learning to play to the camera (right), though she hadn't yet turned to make-up to accentuate her striking features.

the rituals, the kneeling – there's something very erotic about that. After all, it's very sadomasochistic, Catholicism."

"I think maybe the essence of Catholicism I haven't rejected, but the theory of it I have," she told *Vanity Fair* in 1985. "I believe in God. Catholicism gives you an inner strength, whether you end up believing it later or not. It's the backbone."

But whatever the inner strength and backbone gained by the infant Madonna, whatever the erotic connotations and the thrill she experienced when, reportedly, she caught a couple in flagrante in a church vestibule, she was tormented in equal measure by guilt and fear.

Inevitably, when Madonna began her education at the age of five, it was at a Catholic school, the first of three. Initially, she was deeply impressed by the nuns who staffed the establishment, to the point of deciding that she would join the sisterhood herself one day. "I loved nuns when I was growing up," the pupil later reflected. "I thought they were beautiful. I saw them as really pure, disciplined, above-average people. They never wore any make-up and they just had these really serene faces. Nuns are sexy."

There wasn't really anything sexy or serene about the nuns as they routinely doled out slaps and clips in the name of classroom discipline, but Madonna continued to idealise their devotional mystery.

Dodging the devil at every turn, she also remained spellbound by Biblical legend, and, in 1966, picked Veronica as

her confirmation name, after the saint: "I chose her because she wiped the face of Jesus, which I thought was really romantic."

In contrast to the austerity of school and a personal timetable that revolved around church, homework and housework, there were times of great happiness and frivolity within Madonna's family.

Always, there was music around the Ciccones' hearth, and her father urged all of his children to take up an instrument, in Madonna's case the piano. She struggled through her lessons for a year before finally persuading Tony to let her take dance classes instead.

It was Madonna's mother who had ignited her love of dancing, leading by example as she jived around the house to the tune of Chubby Checker. Nonnie thrilled to the exhilaration, watched the steps, and practised alone for hours until she finally felt accomplished enough to offer lessons to her girlfriends.

She was, she remembers, "six-and-a-half or seven" when the mother she adored died from breast cancer, a blow so devastating that she lives with its repercussions to this day, both diminished and empowered by her great loss. She has said: "That period when I knew that my mother wasn't fulfilling her role – and realising that I was losing her – has a lot to do with my fuel for life. It left me with an intense feeling to fill a sort of emptiness."

And, elaborating: "All of a sudden I was going to become

"*I have* my father's *eyes,* but *I have* my mother's smile"

the best student, get the best grades; I was going to become the best singer, the best dancer, the most famous singer in the world. Everybody was going to love me."

She reasoned: "If I hadn't had that emptiness, I wouldn't have been so driven. Her death had a lot to do with me saying – after I got over my heartache – I'm going to be really strong if I can't have my mother. I'm going to take care of myself."

In a 1989 interview, she remarked on the fact that her mother had staunchly tried to grin and bear her illness so as not to frighten the children. "I don't think she ever allowed herself to wallow in the tragedy of her situation. So in that respect, I think she gave me an incredible lesson."

If there was any other "benefit" to be gained from her mother's passing, it was perhaps this: "Not having a mother, while I suffered a great deal from it, also freed me in a lot of ways, as far as thinking what my possibilities in the world would be. Perhaps freed me in terms of the kind of parent that I would be."

Madonna also insisted, grimly, that "Once you get hurt really bad when you're young, nothing can hurt you again."

Yet, beneath the tough outer shell and behind the ruthless determination that supported her quest for fame is a woman who still misses mum and has alluded to her death creatively, notably in the video for 'Oh Father'. "What fuels my ambition is the desire to be heard," she once admitted. "And to find my mother, I suppose." She told *Time* magazine in 1985: "She was very beautiful. I look like her. I have my father's eyes, but I have my mother's smile and a lot of her facial structure."

The Ciccone children were sent to live with various relatives after the death of the elder Madonna, enabling Tony to keep working. They returned to the family home when he hired the first in a succession of housekeepers. Madonna shouldered much of the responsibility for looking after her brothers and sisters, and although she sometimes found this tiresome and restrictive, she took pleasure in the nurturing – a theme which would crop up occasionally in her videos and which she would fully embrace, as a mother herself, with the *Ray Of Light* transformation.

Madonna relished her position as the matriarch of the household. At the same time, she became hugely demanding of her father, returning to the parental bed to snuggle up beside him when she awoke at night, grieving for her mother.

And so it came as a shock to Madonna and her siblings when, three years later, Tony fell in love with one of his housekeepers – Joan Gustafson – and remarried.

"It was hard to accept her as an authority figure and the new number one female in my father's life," admitted Madonna, who told *The Face* in 1985 that Joan was "really gung-ho, very strict, a real disciplinarian".

There's no doubt that Madonna, having now also "lost" her father, was resentful of Joan – and Tony – and outraged at the idea of a substitute mother in the home. Certainly, there was a personality clash, and Madonna became more openly rebellious, more argumentative, outspoken and

prone to fits of temper.

She has claimed that her stepmother would dress the sisters in identical outfits – although Joan says this was never the case. For whatever reason, Madonna started trying to establish her individuality, to create a look of her own, reportedly dressing in multi-colours, customising her clothes by slashing them, and decorating her hair with home-made ribbons and bows. It may well have been her first fashion statement.

By the end of her first year at University, Madonna had decided to relocate to New York to seek fame and fortune. Friends were unsurprised, as she was renowned for her attention-seeking behaviour even back then, though she was an intelligent and grade A student.

Mind the Gap!

There's an old saying that anyone with a gap between their two front teeth is a born singer.

Certainly, Madonna upholds the theory, having displayed a generous space between her top milk teeth as a toddler.

It's interesting that in her general quest for the ideal, she has not pursued cosmetic dentistry but has chosen to make a feature of the endearing imperfection. For impressionists on TV shows, it's just as much a part of the essential look as the Monroe wig or the conical bra, with performers painting in the crucial space. Madonna made only one special effort to bridge that gap, and that was while wearing a mouthpiece for authenticity as Eva Peron in *Evita*.

Elton John's happy-gappy grin is all part of the entertainment for the showman's audiences.

Ray Davies' lazy smile is as memorable as his adenoidal vocals with The Kinks.

Irish singer and goody-two-shoes **Dana** won the 1970 Eurovision Song Contest with 'All Kinds Of Everything' in a voice as sweet and wholesome as her smile.

Red Hot Chili Peppers bassist **Flea** may not sing that often, but he's blessed with the right voice for ranting.

Ray Dorset's sunny smile summed up the feelgood factor of Mungo Jerry's first big hit, 1970's 'In The Summertime'.

Jay Kay has been singing, dancing and smiling all the way to the bank with Jamiroquai.

Out of a Molehill

Perhaps the most fiercely debated aspect of Madonna's appearance is her famous mole.

Some people contend that it does, indeed, exist just under her right nostril, sometimes appearing on the opposite side of her face because a photograph has been flipped and sometimes disappearing when she covers it with make-up – it seemingly vanished during her Earth Mother period. Others argue that the beauty spot began simply as an affectation inspired by Monroe, and that Madonna has since painted it in wherever and whenever she wants.

Back in the Eighties when the mole controversy was at its height, Wayne Hussey, singer with Goth band The Mission, enthused: "I like Madonna having a beauty spot in a different place on every photograph. I love it. I've started doing it too. I've got one by my nipple right now... " Madonna has been known to paint beauty spots on other parts of her face: under her left eye as Marie Antoinette in the MTV 'Vogue' performance; under her right eye for the Cannes Film Festival strip.

Marilyn Monroe the most famous mole of all.

Cindy Crawford's beauty spot has become the supermodel's trademark.

Model **Niki Taylor** makes a mark with a mole at her upper lip.

Janet Jackson leaves nature as it is – unlike her famous brother – with a mole below her left nostril.

Peggy Lee was another blonde with an extra spot of glamour.

Anna Nicole-Smith ensnared the ancient billionaire J. Howard Marshall II with her blonde voluptuousness – and a small mole on her left cheek.

Twin Peaks star **Sherilyn Fenn** makes the most of a beauty mark at her left eye.

Famous gaps (clockwise far left) Ray Davies, Flea, Jay Kay, Ray Dorset, Dana, Elton John. Famous moles (clockwise left) Niki Taylor, Peggy Lee, Sherylin Fenn, Anna Nicole-Smith, Janet Jackson, Cindy Crawford, Marilyn Monroe.

In this early photograph of the Ciccone family, father Tony and stepmother Joan pose with her stepsister and brother, Jennifer and Mario. Madonna found it extremely difficult to adapt to her new mother figure and many have surmised that her career has been built on trying to win her father's approval.

Tony and Joan had two children, Jennifer and Mario, born in 1968 and 1969, and when Madonna was around ten, the expanding family moved to Rochester Hills, Michigan.

Her anger towards Tony continued to fester, although at the same time, she desperately wanted his approval. This conflict of emotions manifested itself in behaviour which would become more outrageous as time went by, apparently intended both to shock her father and test the strength of his love.

Always, she admired him. She told *Time* magazine in 1985: "My father was very strong. I don't agree with some of his values but he did have integrity, and if he told us not to do something, he didn't do it either... That represented a very strong person to me. He was my role model."

At the age of eleven or thereabouts, Madonna scandalised her dad by dancing in a school talent show wearing only a bikini, her body daubed with flourishes of green, psychedelic paint and her long, dark, wavy hair flying wildly as she gyrated. Legend has it that the record playing at the time was by The Who. Madonna was widening her musical appreciation, while still adoring the sweet soul music and female vocal groups of her childhood. Her singles collection included poppy songs such as 'Young Girl' by Gary Puckett And The Union Gap and The Boxtops' 'The Letter', and Nancy Sinatra's classic 'These Boots Are Made For Walking' blew her clean away.

Some British groups were also attracting her interest. She has frequently recalled that when the dancing lessons she gave her girlfriends extended to boys, the single that would go on the record player was 'Honky Tonk Women' by The Rolling Stones – "It was really sexy, right, like stomping and grinding."

Despite being grounded for two weeks, Madonna was encouraged by the bikini episode. At the age of twelve, with all of her awakening hormones in uproar, she paraded a naive but aggressive sexuality for the opposite sex. She left her home conventionally dressed for her parents' benefit, but once out of their line of vision, she tucked her skirts over at the top to shorten them, she flashed her knickers, she slipped on pairs of nylons, she removed her bulky outerwear to reveal tight-fitting outfits that emphasised her already blossoming figure, she

danced furiously at the after-school hops, and she sneaked out to the cinema with boys.

Many of her female contemporaries were appalled, but Madonna was exactly where she wanted to be: out in the lead, provoking, being noticed. Of course, she also wanted to be desired, but she was not about to become the "victim" of the passions she had deliberately aroused in the panting schoolboys. She was therefore unwilling to have sex, although she did reportedly indulge in some light petting with classmate Colin McGregor. He told the *News Of The World* in 1987 that they would slope off for "make-out sessions" among the trees behind the school. She also exchanged a few fumbles with girlfriends staying overnight at her home.

Soon, Madonna was pulling on tight jeans and secretly smoking cigarettes. She was really waging war against her father, but it was a one-sided war for the most part: she staged campaigns that he never saw. Increasingly, she was finding her home life oppressive, with all of its responsibilities and restrictions: "I felt like all my adolescence was spent taking care of babies. I think that's when I really thought about how I wanted to get away from all that."

In May 2001, she told *GQ* magazine: "My father had all these rules and regulations. 'You can't wear make-up, you can't cut your hair, you can't, you can't.' So I went to the extreme... And that just continued, because I was rebelling."

Forbidden to date or go to the movies, Madonna went ahead anyway, and she reportedly participated in the odd shoplifting spree. By the time she was sixteen, her hair was short and dark and she was openly wearing eyebrow pencil and eye liner.

As her rebelliousness grew throughout her early teens, Madonna was also coming into conflict with the Catholicism that, as a pre-pubescent, she had accepted for better or for worse, and the romantic intrigue of the nuns was fading after years of classroom punishment. "I always got in trouble for talking out of turn in school," she told *Time*. "I got tape over my mouth. I got my mouth washed out with soap. Everything."

The nuns had noticed Madonna's emerging sexuality from the earliest moments, and had tried to stamp on it, as did her father, coming down hard on her for her deliberate knicker-flashing. Undeterred, she developed her first crush on a boy called Ronny Howard. "He was so beautiful, I wrote his name all over my sneakers and on the playground, I used to take off the top part of my uniform and chase him around!"

Her next flame was a boy called Tommy. Again removing her upper garments, she mounted her trademark chases and was rewarded with her first kiss, stolen in the convent. It was "incredible", she confessed to *USA Weekend* in 1990.

Madonna's discovery of boys led to serious altercations with the nuns, and marked the beginning of another big disillusionment. "It was at the same time that I started to rebel against religion, to be conscious of what I consider to be the injustices of my religious upbringing," she recalled.

Underlying everything was Madonna's crushing

"I cared *to be* good *at* something... I *wanted to* be *somebody*"

disappointment that a God of love could so cruelly snatch away her mother, a committed Catholic. Now, looking with more probing eyes at organised religion, she could see hypocrisy, misogyny and a tyrannical authority which damaged the lives of everyone it touched even though, in her own case, it had also given strength and courage.

As Madonna struggled with her opposing feelings, she held tight to certain aspects of her religion. She remained fascinated by the drama and ritual of services and the sights, sounds and atmospheres of church interiors, while drawing from Catholicism an appreciation of the family unit and the power of prayer.

Her ongoing love-hate relationship with the church, her dialogue with herself on the journey to spiritual fulfilment, would later become one of the most compelling and theatrically outrageous elements of her work.

But back then as a young teenager, mad with the church, the nuns and her parents, Madonna expressed her internal conflicts in the only way she knew how: "I wanted to do everything everybody told me I couldn't do," she told *The Face* in 1985.

Perversely, then, she appeared in many ways a model pupil after enrolling in Rochester Adams High. She worked diligently, became a cheerleader, took up gymnastics, attended dance lessons to learn jazz and tap, and involved herself in the drama group. Here, she began to learn the art of performance, and to love it. Former pupils and teachers alike remember Madonna as a mesmerising presence onstage, and someone who was clearly bound for glory. They recall, too, how she basked in the applause, sometimes in tears.

Rarely did she pass up the chance of a spot of healthy exhibitionism, particularly if her father was in the audience. Given the opportunity to dance in various productions, she would be as uninhibitedly raunchy as she had been at the after-school hops, while he sat despairing of her bold abandon.

It wasn't just Tony Ciccone who was shocked by Madonna's antics. Many of her schoolmates were, too: typically, she had no intention of *belonging*. As a cheerleader, she showed off her hairy armpits as an emblem of individuality and she wore flesh-coloured tights so that when she raised her skirt, she also raised the eyebrows of anyone watching from a distance.

Once again, her overtly sexual behaviour began to upset the other girls as much as it attracted the boys, particularly when they heard that she had lost her virginity at fifteen to her boyfriend, an older schoolmate – an event she later described, amusingly, as a "career move".

The lucky fellow was one Russell Long, but the experience was perhaps unremarkable. "I still felt like a virgin," she confessed. "I didn't lose my virginity until I knew what I was doing."

"She didn't have a problem with people knowing we were having sex," said Russell years later. "Lots of girls that age would have been embarrassed by it, or would at least not have wanted people to know. Not Madonna. She was proud of it..."

In 1985, she told *Time*: "I remember liking my body when I was growing up and not being ashamed of it. I remember liking boys and not feeling inhibited. I never played little games. If I liked a boy, I'd confront him. I went through this whole period of time when the girls thought I was really loose and all the boys called me a nympho. I was necking with boys like everybody else was. The first boy I ever slept with had been my boyfriend for a long time, and I was in love with him. So I didn't understand where it all came from.

"I would hear words like 'slut' that I hear now. It's sort of repeating itself. I was called those names when I was still a virgin."

Among Russell's memories of those nights with Madonna in the back seat of his "Passion Wagon" – a Cadillac – are long talks about her mother's death and her family. Sometimes, the conversations would take a terrifying turn for the seventeen-year-old Russell. "By the time she was in high school, she was rebelling against (her father) in every way. She seemed so angry at him, though I didn't understand why. She would say, 'What do you think he'd do if he knew we were having sex? Do you think it would freak him out?' And I would say, 'Hell, yeah, it would freak him out.' Then she would come back with, 'Well, then, maybe I should tell him.' I would say, 'Madonna, no! He'll kill me.'

"If she could blow his mind, shock him, she wanted to do it. Even more than that, if she could piss him off, she wanted to do it."

There's no report of Madonna ever bringing Tony such unwelcome news. For all of her attempts to outrage her father, the "other" Madonna wanted nothing more than his love and approval – which fitted in rather neatly with her expressed desire to "show them all".

"I wasn't rebellious in a conventional way," she later recollected, with selective memory. "I cared to be good at something... I wanted to be somebody."

"I wasn't actually the troublemaker in the family," she confirmed to Norman Mailer. "I had a younger sister who was a real tomboy, and my two older brothers were always getting into fights. I went the other way... I was obsessed with impressing my father and manipulating my father, but in a very feminine way. I was obsessed with getting straight As."

Despite her academic successes and her triumphs in the drama group, Madonna professes to have few happy memories of her high school days: "I didn't fit in and that's when I got into dancing. I shut off from all of that and I escaped."

One famous Belly Button

Madonna to *Time* magazine in 1985: "The picture inside the dust sleeve of my first album has me, like, in this Betty Boop pose with my belly button showing. Then when people reviewed the album, they kept talking about my cute belly-button. I started thinking about it and I said, 'Yeah, well, I do like my belly button.'

"I think there are other un-obvious places on my body that are sexy and the stomach is kind of innocent. I don't have a really flat stomach. I sort of have a little girl's stomach. It's round and the skin is smooth and it's nice. I like it..."

She also said, "If a hundred belly buttons were lined up against a wall, I could definitely pick out which was mine. I have the most perfect belly-button. When I stick my fingers in it, I feel a nerve in the centre of my body shoot up my spine."

In 1983, Madonna's belly button was one of very few unadorned parts of her anatomy and was frequently seen during live performances. In April 1994, the star finally customised her stomach, showing off her new belly button ring at the premiere of *With Honors* where she flirted with Indian chic long before 1998's *Ray Of Light*. She fainted when the piercing was done.

Striking a pose in a dance studio in 1983. Dance instructor Pearl Lang remembers that, "I knew she would have trouble being a dancer in any troupe because she was such an individual."

"He used to shout at us that dancing always had to come first"

As Madonna said herself, her teachers at Rochester High remember an industrious and well-behaved pupil, slaving over a hot textbook for those straight As.

While her personal rebellion was of equal importance to the young Madonna, it was usually conducted away from the gaze of authority, and her blows against the empire, considerable as they may have seemed to her, were probably shrugged off as the typical behaviour of an adolescent and quickly forgotten.

Alan Lentz, head of music, said in a *Sunday Mirror* supplement in 2001: "From what I remember, she flourished in the environment here. She was an outstanding actress and a pleasure to teach. The ghetto stuff and the raunchy wild-child image were actually quite a shock. It was all pretty far removed from the pupil we had known at school."

Mary-Ellen Beloat, a former schoolmate and co-cheerleader, has no recollection of Madonna being particularly outrageous at school, although she did have some unusual traits. "She always used to say 'I love you' to me and her other friends," said Mary-Ellen in the Sunday Mirror supplement. "It always seemed a little full-on."

In tenth grade, the year she lost her virginity, something much more significant happened to Madonna. She began attending evening ballet classes with Mary-Ellen – and the instructor, Christopher Flynn, would become the single most influential person in her early career.

"The classes could actually be quite brutal," says Mary-Ellen today. "It was two hours a night and we would carry on dancing until our feet bled. If you did something wrong, Christopher Flynn would hit you with the stick he used to hold to point at things. Or he would stick a pencil between the top of your throat and under your chin to make you keep your head straight while dancing.

"He used to shout at us that dancing always had to come first – before anything else – otherwise we wouldn't get to dance in New York, which was the ultimate accolade."

Madonna rose to the challenge. Inspired by being among serious, classical dance students and thrilled by the encouragement she received from Flynn, she drew on the tremendous capacity for hard work and self-discipline that she had gained from the death of her mother, the teachings of the church and the longing to impress her father. She dropped out of cheerleading to concentrate on her dance training and began a healthy diet to keep in shape.

Madonna told *Vanity Fair* in 1986 that in Christopher Flynn and the dance classes, she had found her niche. "He gave me a sense of culture and style. He was the first homosexual I'd ever known. He opened the door. I said, 'Oh, my God, I've found it.'"

To her great sorrow, Christopher Flynn later died from Aids, She told *Time*: "He saved me from my high school turmoil... I had only studied jazz up to then, so I had to work twice as hard as anybody else and Christopher Flynn was impressed with me. He saw my body changing and how hard I worked. I really loved him. He was my first taste of what I thought was an artistic person. He educated me, he took me to museums and told me about art. He was my mentor, my father, my imaginative lover, my brother, everything, because he understood me."

Christopher said: "She was just a child, but she had a burning desire to learn, that girl. She had this tremendous thirst and, really, it was insatiable."

The first to recognise Madonna's true potential, he gave her confidence, direction and ambition – and he took his underage protege out clubbing around the gay scene. There, she mixed in older, more sophisticated and cultured circles, admired the men's pride in their appearance, soaked up the atmosphere of upfront homosexuality, and delighted crowds of admirers with her devil-may-care dance moves.

As a result of Madonna's entry into dance training and gay nightlife, her behaviour began to change, according to her teachers and classmates. Already on the sidelines of the school's social circles, alongside the archetypal outsiders, she drew further back. She was in a different world now, living out experiences she could not share. She was much happier, more focused, than ever before.

Her French teacher, Carol Lintz, was impressed by Madonna's dancing progress, saying: "Something happened to her at this time, and it caused her to no longer think of dance as a social act, but rather an artistic one. There she would be, in the middle of the dance floor at one of those teen dances, by herself, dancing... I started seeing technique. I started seeing showmanship. It was a fascinating evolution.

"When she graduated, she was given the Thespian Award for her work in the many school plays she did... and she was always the lead... But I never thought of her as an actress. I thought of her as a dancer."

Having excelled in high school, Madonna graduated early, aged seventeen. The key to her next move was Flynn, who'd been appointed to the University of Michigan as a dance professor, and who wanted to take Madonna with him. Nancy Mitchell supplied a reference to support her application for a scholarship in which she described the departing pupil as "extremely talented, dedicated, motivated with a sparkling personality".

Madonna hadn't yet worked out what she wanted to be famous for beyond her childhood dreams of movie stardom, but she realised that dancing was the first step towards whatever it might be. She won the scholarship, made a proud man of her father, and in the autumn of 1976 moved to Ann Arbor to begin life as a dance student. She shared digs in the halls of residence with fellow dance student Whitley Setrakian.

According to Whitley, Madonna never brought any men back at nights. And she never showed any interest in singing, either. Together, they survived on extra dollars earned working in an ice cream parlour – and, according to Whitley, by shoplifting. It was during this era that Madonna claimed for the first time to have scavenged discarded food from bins.

As 1983 drew to a close, Madonna was still experimenting with images, demonstrated by these extremely rare shots of the star devoid of trademark jewellery and opting instead for a simple string of pearls and single earring. Needless to say, this strange blend of primness and glamour didn't last long.

"*My first impression was that I had encountered a force of nature, something that was not completely human*"

Steve Bray

Madonna's dance training was still very much in evidence when Joe Bangay took this photograph (above) of the singer on a trip to London in 1983. This was a brief period in which Madonna's style seemed almost restrained, even if her demeanour was anything but. This rarely seen 1983 shot (opposite) by Joe Morillo shows Madonna trying another early Eighties glamour look. She was cottoning on to the power of skimpy underwear

The sensible haircuts of little Nonnie's schooldays were now a thing of the past: she wore her still-dark hair short and spiky, her eyeliner was becoming ever more dramatic, her eyebrows were plucked into arches and her lipstick was an artform in itself. She chose an equally punky way of individualising her dance outfits. Just as she had slashed her clothes as a child to distinguish herself from her sisters, she was now tearing her tights and her leotards and fastening the rips together with safety pins to become visually separate from her neatly coiffured and dressed contemporaries. "I loved doing things for the shock effect," she later explained.

Throughout her college career, she danced all day, practising and perfecting her classical figures, and danced most of the night too when she hit the clubs, startling the clientele with her overtly sexy displays. In one such spot, the Blue Frogge, she chatted up a local drummer called Steve Bray – a future collaborator. He later recalled, "My first impression was that I had encountered a force of nature, something that was not completely human," and the pair enjoyed a short romance.

At the time, Madonna was rigorously observing a punishing training schedule, and starting to look beyond the campus. Around the time she and some other students performed at a dance festival in Durham, North Carolina, she decided, in collusion with Christopher Flynn, that there was more to life than Michigan, and she intended to find it. She would go to New York.

Believing she had achieved everything possible with her dancing at that level and was ready for new challenges, she saved the tips from her second job as a barmaid to pay for a one-way ticket. "Christopher Flynn encouraged me to go," she enthused later. "He was the one who said I could do it if I wanted to. He made me push myself."

However, in an interview with *i-D* in 1984, she insisted: "When I turned seventeen, I moved to New York because my father wouldn't let me date boys at home. I never saw naked bodies when I was a kid – gosh, when I was seventeen I hadn't seen a penis! I was shocked when I saw my first one. I thought it was really gross."

This was not just a case of selective memory; this was a blatant rewriting of history – a favourite trick of Madonna's.

Clearly, she had seen a penis before she was seventeen. She was almost twenty when she left for New York, she'd been living independently in Ann Arbor for a year and a half before that, and her decision to move was therefore nothing to do with her father's views on dating and everything to do with her own surging ambition.

Tony Ciccone, for his part, was furious at her plans to drop out of university, urging that she finish her studies before launching her quest for fame.

Madonna's response, in July 1978, was to hop on a plane.

"I started wearing bows in my hair

because one day when my hair was long,

New York was where Madonna's game plan finally came together, where she realised how best to hitch her talents to her ambition. By switching her focus to music – a hitherto unexplored territory – she could reasonably hope for fast results and a serious impact. Through a combination of circumstance, design and social influence, she also began to develop the look that would shortly sweep the world like an explosion in a thrift shop.

Everything and everybody that Madonna needed were right there: she only had to find them. Before she did, though, she endured the most poverty-stricken period of her life. She arrived in New York with $35, some dance tights and a good-luck photo of her mother, and at first "relied on the kindness of strangers."

she creates legend."

In Madonna's teenage dream, she would join the multi-cultural Alvin Ailey dance company. In reality, she won a scholarship to its junior company, where for a few months she danced with like-minded wannabes. She also passed an audition with the acclaimed Pearl Lang dance company, where she turned up looking typically punkish, still flying the flag for independence among the leotards.

She told *Time*: "I always personalised (my dance clothes). I'd rip them all up and make sure the runs got really big and had a pattern to them. I started wearing bows in my hair because one day when my hair was long, I couldn't find anything to tie it back, so I took an old pair of tights and

I couldn't find anything to tie it back,

so I took an old pair of tights and wound them around my head,

and I liked the way that looked"

In her first itinerant months, she dragged herself and her few belongings from one dingy bolthole to another, staying with this person and that, just about scraping a living with a succession of dead-end jobs in fast-food joints and money "borrowed" from new friends she made.

Again, she said, she was forced to scrabble through bins for scraps of food. "If I had a dollar to spare, I'd buy popcorn, yoghurt and peanuts," Madonna recalled. "Popcorn is cheap and it fills you up."

Madonna never worried unduly about her standard of living. She thrived on the uphill struggle, and has since remarked, "Life was simpler when I had no money, when I just barely survived." But her lifestyle brought problems: "I'd take a big breath, grit my teeth, blink back my tears and say, 'I'm gonna do it – I have to do it because there's nowhere else for me to go.'"

There was, actually, somewhere else for her to go, and that was home. Tony Ciccone visited Madonna at a time that she was living alone in a building infested by cockroaches and drunks, and begged her, in vain, to return to Michigan.

In 1990, she recalled in *Madonna* magazine: "I'd go to Lincoln Centre, sit by a fountain and just cry. I'd write in my little journal and pray to have even one friend."

Her brother Martin has since dismissed this touching scenario as one of Madonna's romantic revisions. "Oh, please!" he sighs in J Randy Taraborrelli's book, *Madonna: An Intimate Biography*. "She never sat by a fountain and cried. She never wrote in some diary about her loneliness and pain. And she had loads of friends... But she later made it all just a part of the glamorous legend that is my sister. That's what she does best,

wound them around my head, and I liked the way that looked."

"She came in wearing this T-shirt that was torn all the way down the back," Pearl later remembered. "And she had this enormous safety pin, it must have been a foot long, holding it together." Weeks later, Madonna and Pearl parted company after a ferocious row over a dance routine. Lang later commented: "Nothing bothered her. She was going to do something and nothing was going to get in her way."

To solve her cash problems, Madonna modelled nude for art classes, then also for painters and photographers. "You got paid ten dollars an hour," she remembered. "It was a dollar fifty at Burger King."

"I was a dancer at the time," she explained in another interview. "I was in really good shape and slightly underweight so you could see my muscle definition and my skeleton. I was one of their favourite models because I was easy to draw."

On yet another occasion, she proclaimed: "I consider the nude a work of art."

One typical photo session took place in late 1978 at the studio of Bill Stone, who later stated: "I saw that she was special." He didn't realise quite how special. Years later, Bill's photographs would still be selling around the world. As recently as 2001, photographs from the session were still appearing in *Penthouse*.

Stone's photos show Madonna looking thin with modest breasts. Her thick, dark, wavy, almost frizzy hair is touching her shoulders and cut into a fringe at the front. Her eyebrows are shaped and pencilled and although her make-up is visible, particularly eye liner, it's subdued; not tarty.

Madonna later said of the nude sessions: "Obviously I

Still desperately seeking an image, the 25-year-old Madonna poses in the streets of London for Joe Bangay. With shirt buttoned to the collar, only the make-up betrays the glamour queen to come.

Hair
The carefully cultivated haystack – her first famous hairstyle – is a wild, back-combed, streaky tangle of brazen blonde and reddish brown, with green rags tied into the trademark bow at the front.

Eyes
Bright highlighter shines below darkened, bushy eyebrows, while strokes of smoky plum and red shadow, kohl and mascara surrounding the eyes are confidently dramatic.

Beauty spot
Madonna's small mole is accentuated with dark-brown eyebrow pencil – or, if you believe the conspiracy theorists, it's painted on!

Nails
Adding to her multi-colours are greenish-yellow nails, carefully painted to contrast with her familiar, chipped-polish look of the period.

Lips
Fashioned into an angled cupid's bow, this solid, rosy-red shade is darker than her usual favourites but a step towards the later, outrageous crimsons.

Bangles
The vivid flash and sparkle, the cheap and cheerful clutter of her bangles, typify Madonna's 'Borderline' persona, complete with crucifix earring. Guaranteed, her left wrist is adorned with all those famous, black-rubber typewriter bands.

Creating The Look

Hair
Daniel Galvin's "Pop Colour" bob. Sleek, long and "shattered", it is coloured in vertical sections in varying shades of blonde and light brown, blown-dry straight, and treated with special cream for separation and texture.

Eyes
Pale lavender highlights appear below shaped brows, with stronger, violet shadow on the lids and sockets. Mascara, thin liner and false lashes define the eye shape.

Beauty spot
Covered with concealer, foundation and lightly applied powder... or never there in the first place? Whatever, the beauty is frequently without spot nowadays.

Lips
Emphasising her sophisticated, pinkish-pastel facial cosmetics, she sports a Barbie colour, highly glossed, which follows her natural lip line.

Jewellery
The richness of diamonds, presumably real ones, is softened by Madonna's playful personalisations, echoing her customised T-shirts. She may be loaded, but the gal's still gonna have fun, 'cos she's just like us – really!

would have preferred they weren't published, but I think when people saw them they said, 'What's the big deal?' It's other people's problems if they turn them into something smutty. That was never my intention. At first they were very hurtful to me. Now I look back at them and I feel silly that I ever got upset, but I did want to keep some things private. It's not really a terrible thing in the end, but you're not ready for it, and it seems so awful and you seem so exposed."

Blissfully unaware of the controversy in the making, Madonna began dating an artist called Norris Burroughs. She caught his eye at a party where, characteristically, she was cavorting in the middle of the dancefloor to the Village People's disco anthem, 'YMCA', wearing leopard-print pants. That picture is imprinted in his mind as indelibly as the sight of Madonna in a pair of his jeans, several sizes too big.

"She couldn't wait to wear them," he recalled. "She had sweaters and shirts with holes in them and she'd stick her thumbs through the holes, posturing and posing. She always looked cool. She always *was* cool."

In the spring of 1979, Norris threw a party that signalled the end of the line with his cool, denim goddess. That night, Madonna met brothers Dan and Ed Gilroy, who had a band called The Breakfast Club, and fell for Dan. He recollects that she was dressed in something "like a clown outfit".

She moved into the brothers' home in a disused synagogue in Queens, learnt to play several instruments and joined the band, alternating at various times between drums, guitar and vocals. Madonna's old Michigan boyfriend, Steve Bray, caught them in New York. He reported: "With The Breakfast Club, she found her muse medium, she found the best vessel for her drive as a rock performer. She played guitar and fronted the band... She'd dance on the table tops and break things all around her. She'd pour champagne all over herself. She was just a fabulous, wild child."

Having now caught the music bug and seemingly settled

"She *always* looked *cool.* She *always* was *cool*"

Norris Burroughs

into a steady relationship with Dan Gilroy, Madonna suddenly took off again, this time to Paris.

She had answered an ad for girls to tour the world with French disco star Patrick Hernandez. Despite the fact that her knowledge of disco ran to dancing to 'I Will Survive' in New York nightclubs, she attended auditions and was invited by producers Jean Claude Pallerin and Jean Van Lieu to come to Paris where they would make her famous in her own right.

In the event, they gave her everything except the fame that had drawn her to Paris. Madonna travelled to Europe and

Tunisia with Hernandez' entourage, but when she asked what plans were being made for her individually, she was simply given money. The result was a typical Madonna rebellion. She bought clothes to reflect how she felt: leather jacket, jeans and boots, all black. She wore safety pins as earrings. She befriended "lowlifes" and roared around town with a motorbike gang. In short: "I did everything I could to be bad."

After six months of frustration, she flew back to New York, delighted once again to be the mistress of her own destiny. She did some more nude modelling and devoted herself to The Breakfast Club with her customary enthusiasm, practising drums and guitar for hours on end, learning piano, writing songs, singing, rehearsing and promoting the band to anyone she could get to listen.

Around this time she also had her first experience of making a movie, having answered another advertisement. Independent film-maker Stephen Lewicki was about to shoot his own project, *A Certain Sacrifice*, and was looking for actors and actresses for roles including a dominatrix. He had little money, certainly not enough to pay the cast, but Madonna was more than willing to give it her best shot.

Her letter stood out from all the other applications. In it, she told Stephen about her life in intimate detail, and enclosed three photos. One, in which she was applying lipstick with a finger, made up Stephen's mind. Madonna became Bruna the dominatrix, filming her scenes in shoots two years apart, due to Lewicki's cash shortages.

He told Mark Bego in 1985: "She was exactly what I was looking for, this kind of nasty, sexually charged – at the same time vulnerable – female."

The hour-long film, with its scenes of group sex, rape, dismemberment and human sacrifice, was hardly the Hollywood blockbuster that Madonna Ciccone had wished for in her high school daydreams, and it was not an auspicious début. But one of her fellow actors commented afterwards: "She was acting like she had a make-up person and a wardrobe person and a whole entourage, and there was no entourage."

It has been argued, though, that her acting was less self-conscious than would be the case in many of her major movie roles. Joining Madonna in some of the scenes was Angie Smits, who had been recruited to The Breakfast Club as a bassist. Although the two were tight friends early on, Madonna's attitude towards Angie became frosty when she seemed to be winning the lion's share of attention at gigs with her blonde beauty, sexy clothes and provocative stageplay. Madonna spent most of the set at the drumkit, only venturing out front to sing a couple of songs a night.

But the band's career was not shaping up as quickly as Madonna had hoped. It was a struggle to get bookings, and the pay was lousy so, in her usual decisive manner, she left the group and Dan Gilroy, her heartbroken boyfriend. She had made up her mind. She was going to be a singer and, definitely, she was going to be the boss.

Madonna once famously said: "Sometimes I feel guilty because I feel like I travel through people. That's true of a lot of ambitious people. You take what you can and then move on." The next one was Camille Barbone, her first manager.

Madonna had formed a band with her old drummer friend Steve Bray, playing rock music influenced by English groups like The Pretenders and The Police. The colour of her short hair changed with her moods, from shades of red to brown, and it wouldn't be unusual to find her onstage in a pair of man's pyjamas.

They enjoyed various names – The Millionaires, Modern Dance and Emmy, although not Madonna as the singer herself had suggested. She and Bray moved into a block of offices and rehearsal rooms called The Music Building, there to sleep on whatever floor space they could find each night.

Camille Barbone, working there with the Gotham music company, regularly bumped into Madonna, who persuaded her to come along to an Emmy gig. Certain that she had seen a star in the making, Camille snapped her up for management, moved her into a flat, and paid for everything that Madonna wanted, from food to acting lessons, studio time and a bunch of hired hands to record with.

In return, Madonna was asked to observe certain conditions, one being that she mustn't have sex with any of her musicians. If she did, he would be sacked.

Undaunted, Madonna slept with hired hand drummer Bob Riley, who was duly fired, whereupon Madonna demanded that he be replaced by Steve Bray. The alleged incident has long been held up as an early example of Madonna's ruthless behaviour (towards the unfortunate Riley) and willingness to

Music

Madonna's music has changed and matured as certainly as she has, but at its heart, there has always been a fusion of fresh pop and contemporary dance beats, from insistent NYC grooves and hip hop to European trip hop and techno.

Enabling such a mix has been her appreciation and understanding of different types of music from her earliest days.

The sound that first set the young Nonnie's feet tapping was the dance music of its day: the sensational soul music pouring out of places like Tamla Motown and Stax. And although she was big on **Stevie Wonder**, **Marvin Gaye**, **Frankie Lymon**, **Sam Cook** and **Sly & The Family Stone**, she specially liked the female vocalists – **Diana Ross** and **The Supremes**, **The Shirelles**, **The Ronettes** and **Martha Reeves and The Vandellas**. "They're the quintessential pop songs," she decided.

On the opposite side of the Atlantic, girl pop singers including **Lulu** and **Marianne Faithfull** had made their mark on Madonna.

However, the first records that she owned had a very different flavour. They were 'Young Girl' by **Gary Puckett & The Union Gap**, 'The Letter' by **The Boxtops** and 'Incense & Peppermint' by **Strawberry Alarm Clock**. Interestingly, she claims to have been intrigued by **Don McLean**'s original version of 'American Pie', a song she would later take back to the charts.

She says: "It was an important song to me growing up. I distinctly remember memorising every word of it, even though I didn't really know it was about Buddy Holly. I was young, and who cared?"

Moving on up via the earthy bump and grind of the **Stones**, Madonna developed an interest in the classical music that was the soundtrack to her dance lessons, finally finding her niche in the music she heard at the gay, dance clubs she frequented with her instructor and mentor Christopher Flynn.

In 1976 and 1977, Madonna was struck by English punk icons such as **Sid Vicious** – an influence that was apparent in her appearance, if not her music, when the world first heard of Madonna. In New York, she rode the new wave, absorbing the creative energies of **Blondie**, **The Pretenders** and **The Police**.

She said: "My role models were people like **Debbie Harry** and **Chrissie Hynde**, you know, strong, independent women who wrote their own music and evolved on their own, essentially, weren't marketed, produced, put together. They weren't the brainstorm of a record company executive... Debbie Harry gave me courage."

Madonna's wide-ranging appreciation could accommodate the vastly different singing styles of **Ella Fitzgerald**, **Patsy Cline**, **Joni Mitchell**, **Chaka Khan**, **Harry Belafonte**, **Johnny Mathis**, **Joe Cocker**, **Tom Waits**, **Prince**, **Elton John**, **David Bowie** and **Simon & Garfunkel**, to whom 'Oh Father' was a musical tribute.

She would take her inspirations primarily from the sounds of urban club culture and cutting-edge studio producers, but she still carried a torch for grand dames like **Barbra Streisand** who had established successful careers in both singing and acting.

Today, while relaxing to **Mozart** and **Vivaldi**, **Chopin** and **Brahms** in her fabulous homes, the girl who once envied Tammy Wynette's hairdo keeps her eye on the competition and is quick to offer an opinion. Here are some of her comments, many made to Spin magazine.

Eminem "I like Eminem cos I like his attitude and I think he's expressing his anger and I think that's juxtaposed against a lot of what everybody calls kiddie bands. It's refreshing to see somebody who's not trying to be polite and behave the way people want them to behave. I think he's got a lot of spunk and spirit."

Björk "She's incredibly brave and she's got a real mischievous quality about her. I find her very compelling, really daring."

Alanis Morissette (a Maverick artist): "She reminds me of when I first started out: slightly awkward but extremely self-possessed and straightforward... Anything's possible, and the sky's the limit."

Everything But The Girl "There's a plaintive quality to Tracey Thorn's voice that I really respond to. And that song, 'Missing'. I know they've played the shit out of it and I'm over it, but it was such a brilliant song."

Richard Ashcroft "I was into The Verve until 'Bitter Sweet Symphony' was played on the radio every two seconds."

Air "Their album is fierce. I always respond to songs that have a bittersweetness to them, something haunted but with a really visceral groove to it."

Tricky "Have you heard the Stereo MCs' remix of 'Makes Me Wanna Die'? That is a bomb. I like to put that on in my car and play it so loud that my car is vibrating and you can see the doors bending out."

Goldie "I tried to get him to work on one of the tracks from *Ray Of Light*. Nellee Hooper played a bunch of early demos for him and he fell in love with 'To Have And Not To Hold'. We sent him the master tapes and he said he wanted to work on it by himself, and then we never heard from him. Oh well, I guess he was busy."

Fiona Apple "I love the way she sings. I'm attracted to the dark, and she's so dark."

The Spice Girls "I like them. I know I'm not supposed to. Every time someone says something bad about them, I say, 'Hey, wait a minute, I was a Spice Girl once.'" (Madonna has had dinner with both Posh and Mel C.)

Courtney Love "Courtney is such a miserable person. When I met her, when I was trying to sign her, she spent the whole time slagging off her husband. She was saying, 'Oh, Hole are so much better than Nirvana, and just going off on a tangent. She just loves to hear herself talk. She doesn't even mean half the things she says. She's just incredibly competitive with people and anybody who's successful she's going to slag off."

PJ Harvey "I think her lyrics are brilliant. She's real tortured, and I'm drawn to tortured people."

Stevie Wonder "Where is somebody who writes like that now? It's so sad. I can't think of anybody who's as deep and as layered as Stevie Wonder. Instead we get the cartoon version of life: being powerful, rich and having beautiful women. I don't think they are setting out to push the envelope or take music to another level. It's about intention. What are they in it for?"

David Bowie "David Bowie was a huge influence on me because his was the first concert I went to see (Cobo Arena, Detroit, February 29, 1976). I remember watching him and thinking I didn't know what sex he was, and it didn't matter. Because one minute he was wearing body stockings – the whole Ziggy Stardust thing – and the next he was the Thin White Duke in white, double-breasted suits, and there's something so androgynous about him. And I think androgyny, whether it's David Bowie or Helmut Berger, has really influenced my work more than anything."

Influences (clockwise far left) The Ronettes, Debbie Harry, Simon & Garfunkel, Chrissie Hynde, Marianne Faithfull. This page (from top) The Spice Girls, Alanis Morissette, Stevie Wonder, Goldie.

use sex to get what she wanted (Bray in the band).

Madonna had also recognised Camille's bisexuality, and flirted outrageously with her to elicit ever more favours, stepping back when it looked as though Camille would call her bluff. Lesbianism would become a recurring and controversial theme in Madonna's work, and its presence – real or suggested – in her private life would prove an effective weapon, a sure source of controversy in her PR armoury.

Camille, besotted with Madonna, gave her money, professional help and a genuine friendship which was never reciprocated. The pair parted company after bitter rows, with Madonna citing musical differences, wanting to venture into funky, danceable sounds whereas Camille had been steering her into rock.

Back to scraping a living, Madonna found work singing backing vocals for various recording artists but, yet again, she was homeless. Her next move, however, proved crucial, for it was in the East Village that she found the inspiration for the raggle-taggle look with which she would soon bewitch the world of music. It was a sleazy but creative place, throbbing with Puerto Rican culture and filled with hip hop and graffiti art, which caught Madonna's fancy almost as much as the olive-skinned boys.

Accompanied by the new wave friends she made in the Village, she was often out decorating walls and trains with her spray can. She would acknowledge this phase in her 'Borderline' video which includes a spot of breakdancing among scenes where Madonna demonstrates her spray-painting talents and shows off her graffiti name – Boy Toy – on the back of a denim jacket.

Like any self-respecting graffiti artist, Madonna needed a signature. Boy Toy was a provocative nickname which may have implied a saucy, submissive promiscuity but intended something quite different – as she put it, "I toyed with boys". Later, the Boy Toy tag, immortalised on her belt, would become a famous component of her trashy, wild-child persona.

All of that began taking shape in the East Village. Buying second hand, not only because it looked good but because of her limited earnings, she teamed this with that, layered one

thing haphazardly over another, and mixed and matched her colours and fabrics as crazily as she piled on the accessories: belts, hats, fingerless gloves, scarves and stockings, often tied round her head with a bow at the front, and bangles and baubles galore – with lots of naked flesh around the midriff.

She told *Vanity Fair*: "Eventually, when I started becoming an image in pictures, it was the combination of the dance and the ragamuffin and the new wave and this Puerto Recan street style." Years on, she admitted to missing the simple thrill of dressing up, walking round the streets of New York and "seeing the unusual effect I had on people".

Thus attired "for provocation", as she had been in her schooldays, she and her friends – the "Webo Gals" – would go out dancing, and Madonna would always take a tape.

She'd been in the studio several times, once during her time with Camille to record the legendary "Gotham tapes" and, on another occasion, to put down some backing vocals for a German singer, Otto Von Wernherr, a session subsequently released and promoted exploitatively as a Madonna project.

More important was the demo tape she'd recorded with Steve Bray, featuring a handful of songs they'd written together. She'd take copies of a track called 'Everybody' on her girls' nights out, and she conveniently began a romance with Mark Kamins, an influential DJ at the hip Danceteria club, and a would-be producer.

Having persuaded Kamins to play the demo, she took to the floor and shook some serious action. The song, with its call-to-arms dance rhythm, went down the proverbial storm. Kamins told *The Face* in 1985: "Madonna was special. She had her own style – always with a little belly-button showing, the net top and the stockings."

So impressed was he that he set up an introduction to Mike Rosenblatt, A&R man for Warner Brothers' Sire Records. Whatever his views on the tape, Rosenblatt was certainly won over by Madonna in person. He sang her praises over the phone to label boss Seymour Stein who was, at the time, in hospital with heart trouble.

"She had her own style – always with a little belly-button showing, the net top and the stockings."

Mark Kamins

Stein invited Madonna to his bedside and signed her up there and then, smitten by her unique blend of enthusiasm and hard-headed ambition. She was contracted to record two twelve-inch disco singles. The Mark Kamins-produced 'Everybody', released in 1982, hit big in the clubs and the dance chart – without any of the radio stations knowing for sure whether Madonna was black or white.

With this initial success, it came as a shock to Kamins to be dropped from the controls for the next single, especially since Madonna, he claimed, had promised that if he helped her to a record deal, he could produce her first album. It appears she had also promised the production duties to Steve Bray. In the event, she rejected both of her dismayed ex-lovers, and turned to Warners' more famous Reggie Lucas for the second single, 'Burning Up' – another high-scoring hit in the dance world.

In between times, she had met her next conquest – the very hip DJ and remixer Jellybean Benitez – at a club called The Funhouse. With Jellybean as a boyfriend and Warners' dance plugger Bobby Shaw as a champion, Madonna was ideally placed to make top-level contacts and to learn about the industry, which she did – avidly.

She was typically audacious when it came to finding a new manager. "I thought, Who's the most successful person in the music industry, and who's his manager? I want him."

What she wanted, as usual, she got, with a successful audition for Freddy DeMann, who had just parted company with Michael Jackson.

Sire gave generous backing to 'Burning Up', sending Madonna on a series of club PAs where she mimed to the singles. The company also financed a video and hired a stylist and jewellery designer called Maripol, who had helped on the photo sessions for the album. She would become one of Madonna's favourite advisers, and a close friend.

As one person came into favour, so another was on his way out. Madonna wasn't happy with Reggie Lucas' production work on her début album, simply titled Madonna – not least because he had over-ruled her ideas. She therefore recruited Jellybean to remix some of the tracks, with a contemporary understanding and a dash of magic.

It was Jellybean who found 'Holiday' when extra material was needed at the last minute, and it was that song, released as the first single from the 1983 album, that set the Madonna phenomenon in motion as it gradually climbed up Billboard's mainstream Top Twenty.

Next, in 1984, came Reggie Lucas' composition, 'Borderline', which added to the cutting-edge, New York electro-groove an irresistible, Top Ten melody. The accompanying video, beamed into living rooms around the world via MTV, ushered in the era of Madonnamania.

Video was to be a crucial factor in the scale of her success, since appearance and performance were as much a part of the Madonna experience as the songs and the singing; and her developing visual soap opera would be vital to her longevity as an entertainer.

'Borderline' was an opportunity for Madonna to change in and out of lots of outfits, given the photo sessions involved in a storyline which finds her torn between a suave photographer and her regular guy on the street.

With crucifix earrings hanging out from bleach-blonde haystack hair, bracelets clanking and belly-button glimpsed only briefly, Madonna leaps from one shot to another, in colour and black and white, in a riot of leather, lace, denim, fishnet, frills and spills. Her combinations could hardly be freakier, the crop-tops, T-shirts, vests and sweaters jumbled up with cut-off pants, jeans, skirts, ankle socks and high heels, accessorised with belts, hats and her trademark gloves. Notably, she hints at her passion for glamour in a couple of spectacular gowns.

Carrying on with the funky disco of 'Lucky Star', a Top Five smash, Madonna throws her riotous chic together in similarly extravagant style with a few added extras: a more prominently featured stomach, a pair of Raybans, her favourite pedal-pushers worn in tandem with a skirt, cute bootees and a big, star-shaped earring bouncing in time with her dangling, crucifix-laden, silver belts. With her clothes all black, the blazing red lipstick remains a focus, a fascination. Many years later, cosmetics company Laura Mercier would name one of their shades after her.

There was little subtlety about Madonna's make-up in those early days, her eyes ablaze with dramatic strokes of colour, kohl and mascara.

For all of her extraordinary appearance, the 'Borderline' and 'Lucky Star' videos were simple enough illustrations of a vigorous song and dance act which nevertheless introduced Madonna as the girl who probably didn't live next door. She was smart and sassy, bold and sexy, tough and funny, and she had tons of confidence. She was a girl on top, and her look would soon find its way on to the Paris catwalks, courtesy of designers like Christian Lacroix and Karl Lagerfeld.

Some much more sophisticated and outrageous presentations would follow, on video and onstage, and as more became known about Madonna and her methods, her legend would grow.

For now, though, the world just gasped. Thousands of teenage girls improvised their own versions of Madonna's vagabond chic, ripped their T-shirts as eagerly as she had done herself over the years, while thousands of teenage boys dreamed intoxicating dreams.

Madonna went on to sell millions.

Friends

Madonna has a tight circle of friends who reflect her personality rather than her celebrity. She said: "When I started seriously thinking about motherhood and taking care of a child, certain people that I found amusing and interesting didn't seem so terribly amusing and interesting. I did a lot of emotional housekeeping and I wound up with a much smaller handful of friends who are really special and mean a great deal to me. My relationships with them have grown. It's hard to be friends with people who are frivolous when you have an enormous amount of responsibility."

Chris Ciccone (left), her brother, is regularly by her side, as an executive supervising many of her film and video projects and as a good buddy. Like quite a few of her close, male friends, he is gay.

Juliette Hohnen is a friend with whom Madonna spent a lot of time while she awaited the birth of Lourdes.

Ingrid Casares (right), was introduced by her then girlfriend, Sandra Bernhard, to Madonna. The two became close pals very quickly, causing the end of Madonna's friendship with Sandra, and Ingrid went on to co-star in the controversial *Sex* book photos. Madonna's relationship with businesswoman Ingrid, who has owned nightclubs, is as firm as ever.

Rupert Everett, the gay actor, first met Madonna through Sean Penn. He later co-starred with her in *The Next Best Thing* and appeared in her 'American Pie' video.

Sting and Trudie Styler have been loyal and hospitable friends to Madonna, and it was at their home that she met Guy Ritchie. Trudie – who invested in "Lock, Stock... " – is also credited with introducing Madonna to yoga. Sting (left), one of Madonna's early influences, famously said of his fan: "She's outrageous, she's provocative, she's inscrutable. And over the years, we've all been witness to her evolution, from street-smart kid sister to virgin bride, from sex goddess to a yogi. Her mind is as celebrated as her body, she's as feared as she's desired, she leads while others follow... a woman who is all woman, and all women."

Gwyneth Paltrow (right), the Academy-award-winning actress, is as tall as Madonna is short. They make for an odd couple as they get together for yoga sessions, gossipy lunches and wild nights on the town. Their friendship began in 1996 when Madonna sympathised over some intrusive photographs that had appeared in the press. Madonna said at the time: "She's experiencing the upsides and the downsides of being famous for the fist time. That's a lot for someone to take. I wish I could've had someone to turn to at that time in my life."

Guy Oseary is Madonna's partner in Maverick Records.

kdLang, the lesbian singer, is a mutual friend of Madonna and Ingrid.

Donatella Versace (left), became friends with Madonna through the superstar's patronage of the family business.

Rosie O'Donnell, the talk-show hostess, co-starred with Madonna in *A League Of Their Own*, and the pair became close friends. Like Madonna, Rosie lost her mother at an early age. Rosie has Lourdes round to play with her own children and confesses: "She leaves here a totally different child, a candy bar-eating, MTV-watching, spoilt little kid."

Stella McCartney (right), daughter of Beatle Paul, is another designer much admired by Madonna. She created her wedding dress and served as maid of honour.

Sharleen Spiteri, the singer of Texas, buddied up with Madonna when they played together at Brixton Academy. She says: "I'm now close enough to Madonna to call her Madge – but I don't."

Jean Paul Gaultier (left), the outrageous designer, helped Madonna take her wildest steps into cone-cup fashion.

Michael Portillo is perhaps the oddest name in Madonna's little black book. He's friends with Guy's father and stepmother, John and Shireen, who met him as party workers in Portillo's Kensington and Chelsea constituency.

Alex Keshishian, the film-maker, has stayed "in bed with Madonna", just as a good friend.

Debi Mazur (right), the *Goodfellas* actress, goes back a long way with Madonna – to their poverty-stricken existence in New York. Debi says: "We used to run around and go to the Roxy, go dancing and to art shows. At the time, we both had a taste for, you know, Latin boys."

Anna Friel, the actress who made her name with a lesbian kiss in *Brookside*, joined Madonna's circle in 2001 in America. She says: "We hung out a bit. A strong, great woman. I really respect her."

Ali G – not just after the punani!

Niki Harris is a long-serving backing singer, dancer and friend of Madonna's.

"everyone *else* interpreted it as, 'I don't *want* to be a virgin any more. Fuck my brains out!' That's not what I sang at all"

She would complain, in retrospect, that the songs were weak and that it needed more variety.

While the public was loving the fresh danceability of Madonna, the authenticity of its strong, New York City beats, the lady herself was wondering why she hadn't thought to "break out of the disco mould".

Already a step ahead of herself, she couldn't wait to get cracking on her second album, and this time, she wouldn't be pushed about in the studio. She found a kindred spirit in Chic's Nile Rodgers, whose deft production strokes had transformed disco music into something more than a mere nightclub rhythm. David Bowie, Duran Duran, Diana Ross and Sister Sledge were among those who had enjoyed artistic and commercial success with him.

Despite a number of spats in the studio, Rodgers and Madonna shared a clear view of what they wanted to achieve with *Like A Virgin*. Rodgers later enthused: "It was the perfect union, and I knew it from the first day in the studio. The thing between us, man, it was sexual, it was passionate, it was creative... "

While admitting that Madonna could be temperamental, he added: "Everyone told me she was a terrible ogre, but I thought she was great."

As with Madonna, the album was a mix of covers and songs that Madonna herself had a hand in writing. Rodgers introduced a human touch by using a real, live drummer – Chic's Tony Thompson – rather than a machine, and invested the album with a cross-over pop sensibility, a sexy humour and a dynamic musical front.

Some critics felt it too obviously smacked of commercial ambition, but the album and its first single, the title track, both reached Number One shortly after their release in November 1984, and Madonna's dramatisations of the Tom Kelly and Billy Steinberg composition 'Like A Virgin' caused storms of outrage around the world as her reputation gathered a new and controversial clout.

It was hardly Madonna's fault that so many people listened superficially to the lyric, imagining that it detailed or called for an innocent's sexual initiation. While one section of the population huffed and puffed at the scandal of it all, another guffawed heartily at the very notion of a virginal Madonna. Incredibly, she felt she had to explain: "When I did the song, to me, I was singing about how something made me feel a certain way – brand new and fresh – and everyone else interpreted it as, 'I don't want to be a virgin any more. Fuck my brains out!' That's not what I sang at all."

The video, however, was pure Madonna, acting out contemporary visions of "the virgin", bedding her man in a wedding dress and veil, and "the whore", cavorting uninhibitedly in a gondola in Venice, wild-haired, bedecked with chains, studs and a large crucifix, and baring the usual expanse of flesh around her middle. With the hero of the story portrayed as a magnificent male lion, both by a real animal and an actor wearing a mask, and with the closing moments highlighting the singer in an elegant black dress and hat, Madonna's days as a cheap and cheerful video star were over. She was moving into serious spectacle.

The symbolism of the wedding dress was pretty straightforward in the video, but Madonna wasn't finished yet. She would take things further by perverting the "chaste" connotations of the traditional garment.

She'd already done it once, in front of the world's cameras at the first annual MTV Awards in September 1984, before the album and single had been released. Premiering 'Like A Virgin' in an outfit organised by Maripol (who also styled the album sleeve), she stood on top of a massive wedding cake dressed all in white, the purity of her wedding finery perfectly compromised by the famous Boy Toy belt buckle and the jangling, clanging jewellery – and by Madonna's subsequent thrashing around on the stage floor while a cameraman filmed where the sun don't shine.

Taking the concept out on the road in spring 1985 for "The Virgin Tour", with the up-and-coming Beastie Boys supporting, she changed every night into a sparkly, white bride's outfit for a finale of 'Like A Virgin' and 'Material Girl'.

There was thunderous applause as she returned to the stage, carrying a wedding bouquet, in a midriff-exposing top and billowing skirt, a short jacket, a train, a stole, the ever-present cycle pants, a white bow atop her hair and lacy, three-quarter length gloves. A crucifix glittered at her waistband while another hung from her neck, and balloons floated out to the audience as she crawled and rolled around the stage.

During 'Material Girl', she stripped down to her boob tube and a tight white skirt, throwing scores of Madonna bank notes to the front rows, declaring, "I don't need money, I need love!"

As she began to strip off even more clothes at the climax of the set, she was apprehended and marched offstage by an extra posing as her father; in Detroit, Tony Ciccone himself did the honours. She told a *Time* reporter during the tour: "I think now he has some conception of my success. It wasn't until my first album came out and my father started hearing my songs on the radio that he stopped asking me questions. My father and I are still close."

Two other costumes appeared during "The Virgin Tour", neither so memorable. Madonna entered to a great fanfare wearing a blue see-through crop- top revealing the customary black bra, a purple skirt, lacy leggings and a brightly patterned jacket, with the crucifixes on her jacket, her ear and around her neck catching the light as she danced.

"I guess you could call what I wear sportswear for sexpots," said Madonna in 1985, referring to the work-out T-shirts she would crop and wear with lacy undergarments. This particular photo session went on to grace the cover of *Penthouse* when early nudes of Madonna were published in September '85.

"Will you marry me?" Madonna asked the adoring crowd as she appeared in full bridal attire to sing the first encore, 'Like A Virgin' before flinging her bouquet into the audience. Although the crowd bayed "yes", Madonna was already engaged to Sean Penn whom she would marry a matter of months later. When tickets for Madonna's Virgin Tour went on sale, all 17,622 seats for her three Radio City performances sold out in 34 minutes, setting a new record for speedy sales. She would repeat this feat sixteen years later when the Drowned World tour dates were announced.

IRGIN

For What It's Worth . . . .

Madonna has recently taken to telling people that "I kind of forget that I have money sometimes," and has become "puritanical" about her spending – perhaps in line with her entry into upper-class, English circles where shows of wealth are viewed with disapproval.

Madonna's personal fortune is inestimable, although she's frequently described as the richest woman in America and the latest guess puts the Ritchies' combined earnings at £150 million.

Anything to do with Madonna or her name will generate thousands. The lucky photographer who happens across a topless Madonna on a beach with Guy is looking at a £100,000 payday.

In March 2001, Irish comedian Graham Norton spent £10,000 on a Herb Ritts photograph of Madonna's eyes, which she had taken off her wall and donated to a celebrity auction in aid of Aids charity Crusaid. Norton said: "I'm going to hang it over the bed so she can watch me."

Several months later, bidders splashed out even bigger sums of money to own some of the star's legendary costumes. At an online auction jointly held by Sotheby's and New York shop Gotta Have It!, the beaded Dolce & Gabbana bra she wore on "The Girlie Show" went for $23,850, while the famous tasselled bustier from the "Who's That Girl?" tour fetched $20,550, matching the price paid earlier in the year for a black-satin, conical bra worn on the "Blond Ambition" tour.

Also under the hammer: the "Who's That Girl?" black and gold gloves ($5,000) and the jewelled "Dame Edna" spectacles ($4,200), the John Galliano Forties suit from the 'Take A Bow' video ($13,800), a Gaultier lace gown ($11,212) and a pair of shoes from *Evita* ($3,565).

The handwritten lyrics to 'Like A Prayer' brought in $20,000, an MTV award for 'Express Yourself' sold for $11,500 and the platinum record for 'Like A Virgin' cost someone $5,175. A set including a four-track demo tape, CV and rejection letter from Millennium Records realised $6,037.

Close to her Heart

Champion of the condom, Madonna's longest and best-known campaign is for Aids awareness, safe sex and sexual responsibility, although she has also vigorously protested at the destruction of the rainforest and world hunger. She has stood up for individual rights and choices and self-expression, and promoted equality for gays and women. She has also urged the public to use their votes.

On September 11, 2001 when two passenger airliners crashed into the twin towers of the World Trade Centre, Madonna was playing the American leg of her "Drowned World" tour. She immediately pledged the profits from her September 13 show at the LA Staples Centre to the children orphaned by the terrorist strikes.

During that show, she wore an American stars and stripes flag as a skirt, and held a silent prayer for the victims of the catastrophe.

Existing speculation that Madonna would stop touring after "Drowned World" increased, with travellers' general loss of confidence in the safety of flying.

Madonna is frequently involved in charitable work. Having lost a number of close friends including Martin Burgoyne and ballet teacher Christopher Flynn to the devastating illness, her favourite cause is AIDS research. Here (left) she takes part in a benefit LA Danceathon.

"*Crucifixes* are sexy *because* there's a *naked* man *on them*"

Rattling a tambourine in time with her two male dancers during 'Into The Groove', with the trio adopting matching, white-trimmed trilby hats for 'Everybody', she changed for 'Gambler', 'Lucky Star', 'Crazy For You' and 'Over And Over'. Now she was all in black – her fringed micro-top and skirt exposing the familiar tummy-button, and crucifixes ranging in size from average to big to massive.

Before long, Madonna would launch her own Wazoo clothing label selling Boy Toy belt buckles, crop-tops, T-shirts, rubber bracelets and all the other trappings of her chaotic, gypsy clutter in department stores across America. Young female fans would spend any amount of time and money on looking like their heroine. Fredericks of Hollywood, a leading lingerie store, would later credit Madonna and her brazen concept of "underwear as outerwear" with a forty per cent increase in sales.

By now, the fame that Madonna had worked so long and hard to achieve was making it impossible for her to live a normal life. She could no longer walk the streets of New York, go shopping or clubbing with friends, or sit down to dinner in a restaurant. Everywhere, there were people flashing cameras and demanding autographs. She could hardly complain: she'd wanted all of it.

She had also become something of a hate object in certain quarters, not least among establishment figures who were offended by her "sacrilegious" flaunting of crucifixes and rosary beads in a thoroughly unholy setting. She enraged these authorities even more with flippant retorts, including the notorious quip to *Penthouse* in 1985: "Crucifixes are sexy because there's a naked man on them." Turning the corner, she told the writer that the crucifixes in her childhood home served as "a reminder that Jesus Christ died on the cross for us."

It could be argued that the crucifix, for Madonna, represented both of her conflicting views of Christianity – quite apart from the fact that it was a brilliant gimmick and a springboard for columns of colourful publicity.

Meanwhile, Madonna's reputation for ruthlessness began to grow. She later commented, "Sometimes you have to be a bitch to get things done..." and added: "I'm tough, ambitious and I know exactly what I want... if that makes me a bitch – OK!"

Targeted for being "tarty" and "sleazy", Madonna pointed out that the sexy antics of male rock stars never met with any disapproval. In another instance of gender inequality, she complained that she had to be work hard to be taken seriously by the Warner executives, who couldn't quite accept that the naughty blonde bombshell might also have a sharp brain and a deadly ambition.

One insult rankled more than any other. The hoopla surrounding Madonna often acted to obscure her serious endeavours, and she was furious to be branded a flash in the pan, in the media and among some of the label staff. Years later, she would still feel the sting, remarking: "Everyone agreed that I was sexy, but no one would agree that I had any talent, which really irritated me."

In the flush of her new star status, Madonna left Jellybean Benitez, amid tales of infidelities on Madonna's part. Jellybean has put many of the problems down to "egos, man", and busy schedules, with both careers on the rise. Later, with Madonna flying higher, up, up and away, he said of the split: "We had gone through changes just like any other couple."

Jellybean was another of her so-called "career" boyfriends, but he, like the others before him, shows no malice towards his former lover. Realising her career drive came before everything, he seemed to support Madonna's theory: "All the men I stepped over to get to the top... every one would have me back because they all still love me and I love them." She has elaborated: "If anyone wants to know, I never fucked anyone to get anywhere... Everyone thinks I'm a nymphomaniac, but I'd rather read a book."

In 1984 Madonna had accepted a role in the movie *Desperately Seeking Susan*. Director Susan Seidelman had followed a gut instinct to sign her, but contrary to publicity about a cosy friendship between Madonna and Rosanna Arquette, the star of the film, there was tension between the two as Madonna's fame exploded during the filming. An engaging, "trading places" comedy set in New York, it earns its laughs from the confusion of Arquette's bored housewife who bangs her head and wakes up believing she is the itinerant, streetwise Susan.

Rush-released in 1985 to capitalise on Madonna's enormous success, and featuring 'Into The Groove' on its soundtrack, it fulfilled one of the young Nonnie's dreams, to become a film star. To that end, she was punctual and disciplined on the set. That she emerged with such credit is generally attributed to the fact that rather than acting, she played herself: a spunky, sparky, rock'n'roll hustler. In one scene, her boyfriend Jimmy strikes a chord with the line: "She plays with people."

Madonna suggested that while she was focused on her career, her character was a rootless individual, but she added: "I shared a lot with Susan. She's a free spirit and she says and does what she wants. She's a clever con artist and she doesn't let you know when you're being conned."

Many of the clothes in the movie were her own. Madonna was immediately identifiable with her bare midriff, the scarf-bows, the pedal pushers and the see-through tops over a reliable black bra, and she wore the usual array of crucifixes, necklaces, earrings, and bangles, including the typewriter parts that she used as rubber bracelets.

She consulted with the costume department, rejecting outright their ideas for vintage clothes. Eventually, they agreed on combinations: "I put together things, like one outfit will be my shirt, their skirt, my socks, their shoes."

Madonna's look for the Virgin Tour was deliberately provocative, consisting of lacy bras worn under skimpy tops which would frequently ride up to give a brief glimpse of the Material Girl's breasts (opposite). For 'Gambler' (below), she donned a black tasselled number with shades and waistcoat while gyrating against a pole and crawling through her guitarist's legs. The face of rock'n'roll would never be the same.

SUSAN

The relationship between Madonna and Rosanna Arquette was reportedly strained during filming, Arquette taking umbrage when one of Madonna's new demos – a cut called 'Into The Groove' – was integrated into the movie. "I told them that if *Susan* was going to be a two-hour rock video spotlighting Madonna, well, I didn't want to be a part of it," said Arquette later.

Susan's image in *Desperately Seeking Susan* was created by Madonna herself, who supplied her own clothes and jewellery for the role. In one scene she even wears a jacket emblazoned with MC – though this supposedly stood for the Magic Club central to the film's finale, most didn't miss the fact that these were also Madonna's initials.

The Hollywood Dream

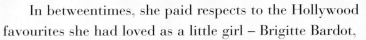

She borrowed from Dietrich, she stole from Minnelli and she revamped almost everything Monroe had to offer.

In betweentimes, she paid respects to the Hollywood favourites she had loved as a little girl – Brigitte Bardot, Grace Kelly and Ann-Margret – and to the other great names that inspired her as she pursued her career: Greta Garbo, Bette Davis, Judy Holliday, Carole Lombard, Lana Turner, Deborah Kerr, Veronica Lake, Sophia Loren and Elizabeth Taylor, who became a personal friend.

In more recent times, she admired the work of Jessica Lange, Charlotte Rampling and Susan Sarandon (and in dance/choreography, Martha Graham – "she was always the aggressor who trapped the men"), and has had complimentary things to say about directors Bob Fosse, Martin Scorcese, Jamie Foley, Francis Ford Coppola, Roman Polanski and Mike Nichols.

She has declared her favourite films to be *A Place In The Sun*, *To Kill A Mockingbird*, *The English Patient*, *East Of Eden*, *Last Tango In Paris*, *Casablanca*, *The Night Porter* and *Breathless*.

As a student, Madonna delighted in the "cool film programme" she was exposed to, including the French cinema of Jean-Luc Godard and Italian works by Pasolini, Visconti, DeSica, Fellini and Antonioni. She said: "With Pasolini, there's religious ecstasy intertwined with sexual ecstasy, and when I think of Visconti's films, I always feel sexually confused by them."

Movies have, of course, brought influence to bear on every aspect of her work, even songs. She has said that 'Frozen' was inspired by the film *The Sheltering Sky*, adding that she loved "that whole Moroccan-orchestra-super-romantic-man-carrying-the-woman-he-loves-across-the-desert vibe. I wanted something with a tribal feel, something really lush and romantic."

But always, there's Marilyn.
"Marilyn Monroe was my first movie idol," she has said.
"When I saw her and Brigitte Bardot, I wanted to make my hair blonde and wear pointy bras..."

Certainly, she managed that.

Here is a little more of what Madonna has had to say about the actress who directly inspired so much of her imagery.

Hollywood heroines
(clockwise far left) Liza Minnelli,
Elizabeth Taylor, Brigitte Bardot,
Marlene Dietrich.
This page (clockwise from top left)
Madonna and Marilyn Monroe .

"I love dresses like Marilyn Monroe wore, those Fifties styles really tailored to fit a voluptuous body."

"I'd love to be a memorable figure in the history of entertainment in some sexual comic-tragic way. I'd like to leave the impression that Marilyn Monroe did, to be able to arouse so many different feelings in people."

"Marilyn was made into something not human in a way, and I can relate to that. Her sexuality was something everyone was obsessed with, and that I can relate to. And there were certain things about her vulnerability that I'm curious about and attracted to...

...she has a beautiful, fragile, childlike quality."

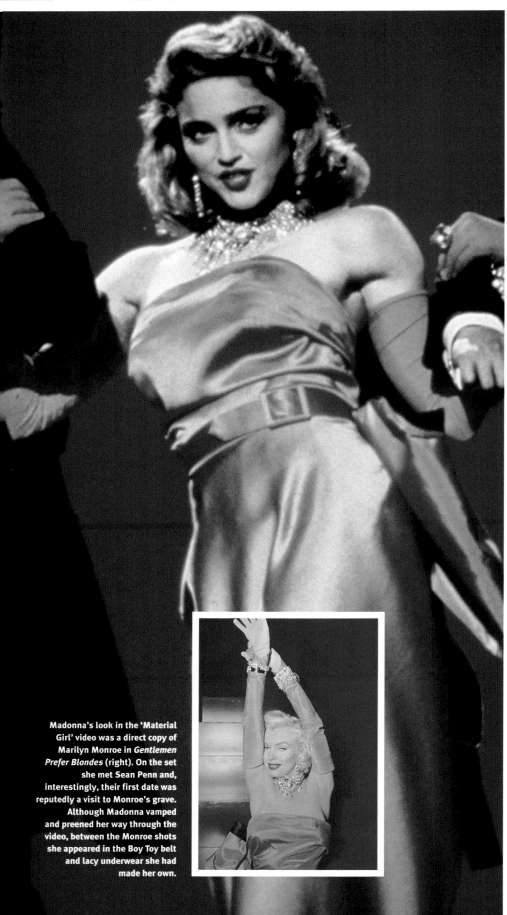

Madonna's look in the 'Material Girl' video was a direct copy of Marilyn Monroe in *Gentlemen Prefer Blondes* (right). On the set she met Sean Penn and, interestingly, their first date was reputedly a visit to Monroe's grave. Although Madonna vamped and preened her way through the video, between the Monroe shots she appeared in the Boy Toy belt and lacy underwear she had made her own.

A much more glamorous affair was the video for 'Material Girl', filmed at the beginning of 1985. Here, Madonna dressed up as Marilyn Monroe like the starstruck little girl she once was, thrilling to old movies in her few permitted hours of television viewing. Teaming up again with 'Borderline' and 'Like A Virgin' director Mary Lambert, Madonna re-enacted the scene from the classic *Gentlemen Prefer Blondes* in which Monroe danced her way around 'Diamonds Are A Girl's Best Friend'.

With an obvious lyrical link – and Madonna proclaiming that her take was intended ironically (an unconvincing argument, with hindsight, although she does end up with the "poor" guy in the video) – she took the visual aspects to the extreme, appearing in a recreation of Monroe's glamorous pink ballgown, complete with massive bow at the back, long evening gloves, a snuggly, white stole, diamond jewellery, curled, honey-blonde hair, perfectly copied make-up... and a flash of crucifix earring in the final scene, lest we forget...

Watching her performance on the video set was a man who was interested in meeting her: the Bratpack hellraiser Sean Penn.

Around this time, Madonna was reputedly enjoying brief romances with Prince and a session musician called Tommy Quinn. But she responded to something "reckless, adventurous" in Penn, and began a roller-coaster romance with the intense and volatile actor.

She later reflected: "Why I fell for him that day, I can't say... I just know I wanted him."

AL GIRL

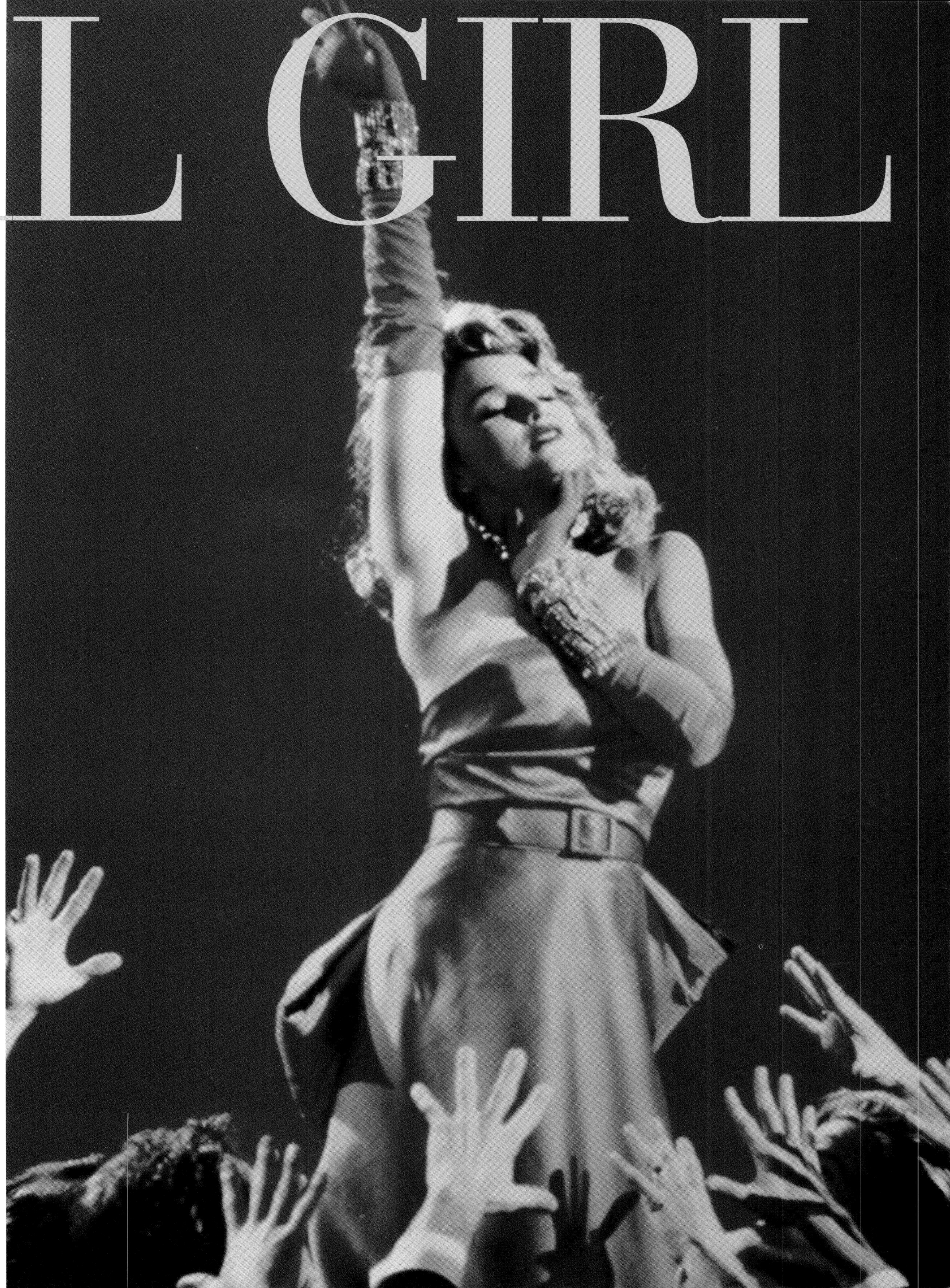

The Celebrities

WhatTheySayAboutMadonna...

Mel C "Madonna was doing the Girl Power thing a long time before the Spice Girls were around. I was definitely one of the wannabes. I had the lace, fingerless gloves, wore silly odd socks and poncey little boots, and I've still got a lot of crucifixes, actually... 'Express Yourself' is one of the routines that I know and I used to really like doing that one because it is where she shows her bra and holds her crotch... really dominating over the boys. She's always got wicked videos...

"The first time I met her was in New York in 1998. She'd invited me out to dinner... I was quite nervous about meeting her, but she's got this air about her that makes you feel very easy in her presence."

Kylie Minogue (right) "I wonder how much that would cost – an ad on Madonna's breasts? It would be pretty expensive, so I was really taken aback. I was really floored by that. It's like being blessed by the Pope...

"Her ability to move with the times and the strength of her convictions is something unusual in pop music, where things are usually so transient. She mixes things that we know and understand and then completely repackages them. No one else can package things like that and we are hoodwinked into thinking, God, that is brand new."

H from Steps "I couldn't believe it when she was on the same bill as us on *Top Of The Pops*. She brushed past me in the corridor and said, 'Hi.' I don't think I'd been that excited for ages. I couldn't speak!"

Faye from Steps, at the "Drowned World" London show: "We do shows in big places and they're quite elaborate, but then you see something like that and you just think, Hmmmm. I have to take my hat off to that lady. This is the ultimate show I've seen in my life so far.

"She's putting less emphasis on her face this time. In the past, her face and her make-up were her identification, her stamp. Now it seems the overall image you can see right across the stage is more important... It seems like she doesn't need that mask any more . . .

"When I was growing up, Madonna was such a clear picture of a strong woman. Now, she's still something to aspire to... "

Don McLean (left), composer and original singer of 'American Pie': "I have heard her version and I think it is sensual and mystical. I also feel that she's chosen autobiographical verses that reflect her career and personal history... I have received many gifts from God, but this is the first time I have ever received a gift from a goddess."

Britney Spears (right) "I have been a huge fan of Madonna since I was a little girl. She's the person that I've really looked up to. She's very independent and doesn't care what other people think. That's very empowering for teenagers, and women in general... I would really, really like to be a legend like Madonna. Madonna knows what to do next and when she's performing, the audience is just in awe of her... Her choreography definitely opened the door for girls to go in there and do their own thing."

Bob Guccione, *Penthouse* publisher: "A great number of Madonna nudes surfaced at once and we had first choice. They came from many different sources – photography teachers and their students, amateurs and professionals."

Cerys Matthews of Catatonia "I've got respect for the lady and she's writing from the heart a lot more. I didn't like her voice, but now she sounds like she's got soul."

Luciano Pavarotti (right) "It is my hope (to sing with Madonna). Madonna has a very clear idea. She promised me to come if we could sing together 'Caro Mio Bene'."

Caprice, model, celebrity and failed pop star: *"As an artist you've got to evolve – just look at Madonna."*

Usher "I can honestly say that I use her career as a map of where I can go. I really admire the fact that she's been able to act, dance, write, produce, own her own record company and have such a great career. And she has become a beautiful person."

Kim Gordon of Sonic Youth "She's so strong, beautiful and manipulative. All of which means she writes great songs."

Martin Amis, writer: *"She is the self-sufficient post-modern phenomenon... a masterpiece of controlled illusion."*

Debbie Harry "She's an aggressive person to achieve anything like she's achieved. Her lyrics are not, 'Hit me again, I love it.' They're more, 'Come here baby, this is it.' She's very timely, she's right on time."

Suzanne of Hear'Say "As a kid, my best memory of her was when she did 'Holiday'. I dressed up in polka dots, a tied shirt and danced around to her music."

Chrissie Hynde "Sean Penn asked me never to see Shanghai Surprise. He said, 'As a friend, don't watch it.' So I never will."

George Michael (left) *"In many respects she's the perfect pop artist."*

Lil' Bow Wow "I accompanied her to the Grammys this year (2001). She just called me up and asked if I wanted to go with her. When you get a call like that, you don't need to think twice about it."

Gem Archer of Oasis, at the "Drowned World" London shows: "I didn't come out to see four naked blokes hanging from the roof on strings."

The Beverley Sisters "As the Beverley Sisters, we were banned by the TV bosses from wearing our daring dresses more than thirty years ago. So you can tell Madonna and the rest that they didn't discover the belly button!"

J from 5ive *"She doesn't have any financial worries now, so she should just enjoy the fact that she's alive."*

Jacqueline Stallone, mother of Sylvester: "Madonna and Sean Penn looked like they needed a bath and a flea-dip when I saw them in a restaurant. Her clothes were shabby and she had no make-up on."

2: THE REALISATION **1985–1993**

It was time to say goodbye to the first phase of her career, and to the trampy, raggedy image she had sold to the world.

Madonna was about to discover the power of costume as opposed to clothes, and would begin to master the art of reinvention which, combined with her natural aptitude for surprise and outrage, a steely determination and her long-serving work ethic, would drive her career through to the Millennium, and beyond.

Finishing the triumphant "Virgin" tour, Madonna faced another barrage of publicity. Sean Penn, filming in Nashville, Tennessee, made the first of his notorious assaults on photographers when Madonna came visiting. He later received a ninety-day suspended sentence and was fined $100 for the misdemeanours.

No sooner had Madonna announced their engagement, in Los Angeles in June 1985, than *Playboy* and *Penthouse* exploded on to the news stands with different naked Madonna spreads, bought from photographers she had posed for as she scraped a living in New York: Bob Stone, Martin Schreiber and Lee Friedlander.

Her embarrassment stemmed from the exploitation and her own helplessness in the situation, and not from the images themselves. No shrinking violet, Madonna would later pose naked with a sheet – and a lot more style – for *Vanity Fair*, and she would take things a lot further than nudity in her own *Sex* book.

couple's elaborate attempts to keep the details secret, helicopters appeared overhead in the hours leading up to the wedding while Penn fired a pistol at them, and photographers were ejected from their hiding places in the grounds of friend Kurt Unger's Malibu mansion, where the wedding took place on a cliff top.

Families, friends and members of the Hollywood elite had their finery blown about by winds from the chopper blades as Madonna took her vows in a fairytale dress, a low-cut, white, strapless creation by Marlene Stewart. The skirt, made from layers of tulle and a sash, fashioned from pink, silk net, was decorated with jewels and dried flowers. To complete Marlene's efforts towards a "Fifties feeling, something Grace Kelly might have worn", Madonna finished the outfit with a veil attached to a black bowler hat.

The "Poison Penns", as they quickly became known, went on to co-star in the universally panned film, *Shanghai Surprise*, produced by George Harrison's Handmade films and later described as "one of the worse movies ever made". It was a role for which Madonna toned down her appearance, inspired again by Monroe, with her hair golden-blonde, waving or curling gently down to her shoulders, her dresses usually in Thirties style and her junk jewellery back in the drawer.

It was no coincidence that Maripol's retail business went bankrupt shortly afterwards.

Madonna held that look for the "Live To Tell" video, predicting the arrival of her new album, *True Blue*, which she

Taking to the Philadelphia stage for Live Aid in July 1985, just days after early nudes were published in *Playboy* and *Penthouse*, a newly brunette Madonna defied expectation by wrapping up in the summer sun. "I ain't taking shit off today," she told the expectant crowd. "You might hold it against me ten years from now."

"I ain't taking shit off today!"

With the battle of the billboards still creating shockwaves, an ill-tempered Madonna appeared at the Philadelphia leg of the giant, money-raising Live Aid concert on July 13, and was later said to be the only performer to behave like a prima donna. Onstage, she teased the audience: "I ain't taking *shit* off today!", in reference to the nude photo scandal. She later recalled: "I decided to be a warrior and it worked, and that was the first time that I really understood my power."

Indeed, the chestnut-haired Madonna seemed perhaps a little over-dressed, with a brocade jacket hanging over a long waistcoat, a short, flowery top and a pair of loose, rose-patterned trousers. As ever, her jewellery caught the eye, with a clutter of necklaces, including a CND symbol and the compulsory crucifix, trailing down over the celebrated, bare stomach and a large brooch pinned, dramatically, near her lapel.

With another controversy – the release of Stephen Lewicki's film, *A Certain Sacrifice* – keeping her publicity profile high, she married Sean Penn on her birthday, August 16, amid unprecedented scenes of media determination. Despite the

had mostly co-written and, with growing confidence, had co-produced with her old boyfriend Stephen Bray and keyboardist Pat Leonard.

Showing clearly that she viewed herself more as a technicolour creation than a pop singer, Madonna explained: "In pop music, generally, people have one image. You get pigeonholed. I'm lucky enough to be able to change and still be accepted. If you think about it, that's what they do in the movies; play a part, change characters, looks and attitudes. I guess I do it to entertain myself."

And then she chopped off her hair. Emerging with a blonde, feathery, pixie cut for the video accompanying 'Papa Don't Preach', released in June 1986 along with the album, Madonna looked young, almost boyish, newly natural, having dispensed with the old, theatrical make-up in favour of softly smudged eye shadow and a subtle lip shade.

She told *Vanity Fair*: "Obviously, if you spend a couple of

Introduced by Bette Midler as "a woman who pulled herself up by her bra straps and has been known to let them down occasionally", Madonna later admitted, "Before I went on, I really thought, 'I can't do this'." But despite private insecurities Madonna gave a characteristically charismatic performance. "That was the first time that I really understood my power."

"I act out of instinct, just like an animal ... That image had to be cleaned thoroughly"

Tired of the heavy jewellery and make-up, Madonna chose the 'Papa Don't Preach' video, released in June 1986, to unveil a new, sleek, gamine image (below). Talking to the *New York Times*, she described her new look as "very innocent and feminine and unadorned. It makes me feel good." The controversial video also saw Madonna pay tribute to her Italian roots (opposite), wearing a cheeky T-shirt that, unsurprisingly, became a big seller in Italy.

years wearing lots of layers of clothes and tons of jewellery and it just takes you forever to get dressed and your hair is long and crazy, then you get the urge to take it all off and strip yourself down and cut your hair all off just for a relief."

She added: "I act out of instinct, just like an animal... That image had to be cleaned thoroughly."

The video finds Madonna in a leather jacket variously matched with jeans, a stripey top, a T-shirt and a flared Fifties skirt, although she hints at something a little racier for the future in the dancing sequence. Here, with her hair sprung into curls, her lips red and her eyes colourfully glossed and outlined, she wiggles temptingly in skintight, black pedal pushers, wide belt and bustier. We didn't know it then, but it was the start of the corsets and the big bras!

The T-shirt bearing the legend "Italians Do It Better" has become an instantly recognisable Madonna garment, resurrected by Dolce & Gabbana as recently as 2000 in a collection inspired by Madonna through the ages. Her taste for displaying messages on clothes followed a direct line from her early dabbling in graffiti art and "Boy Toy" sloganeering to the personalised T-shirt craze she kickstarted in 2000.

In "Italians Do It Better", she was celebrating both her own identity and a liking for certain men, having frequently made statements such as: "I dig skin, lips and Latin men... I guess a lot of my hot-blooded and passionate temperament is Italian. I like dark, brooding men with rough tempers. Italian men like to dominate and sometimes I like to cast myself in the submissive role."

Her use of the expression "cast myself" is telling and typical. As a hit single, 'Papa Don't Preach' created a stir withits story of a pregnant girl opting to have her baby. Although Madonna didn't write the song, she saw it as a simple piece of storytelling about "a girl who is making a decision in her life".

Madonna played the kooky but streetwise Nikki Finn in *Who's That Girl*, adopting an image that was half Betty Boop, half Marilyn Monroe (right). The film bombed, Madonna herself opining in February 2000, "I think all of it was pretty bad." For the 'La Isla Bonita' sleeve (far right), Madonna flirted with a Spanish image, complete with embroidered bolero jacket. The pictures would later be used for the Who's That Girl tour promotion and the *You Can Dance* remix album, issued in November '87.

No one was more horrified than Madonna when pro-life groups applauded the lyric and feminists took offence, both believing that it adopted an "anti-abortion" stance. In another interpretation, moral campaigners complained that it encouraged teenage pregnancy. "I don't have any banner to wave," argued Madonna. "I just wanted to make this girl a sympathetic character."

She looked equally fresh in the 'True Blue' video, flashing back to Fifties' rock'n'roll youth culture, but her next creation – a peep-show stripper – was a jaw-dropper. Writhing extravagantly around a chair to 'Open Your Heart' with sly winks to Marlene Dietrich and Liza Minnelli, she comprehensively introduced the fantasy sex garb most immediately linked to her name; the type that girls would choose to this day should they go to a fancy-dress party as Madonna.

Squeezed into a Marlene Stewart, tight, black basque with gold-tipped, pointy cups and tassels, sparkly black and gold three-quarter-length gloves and fishnet tights, she peels off a short, sleek black wig to reveal white-blonde hair.

Capricious as ever, she finally defuses the highly charged atmosphere of the video with a twist of humour, dancing out of the building and into the distance with a lovestruck little boy. The clip, directed by Jean Baptiste Mondino, also marks Madonna's first video depiction of homosexuality – a recurring fascination – with a sailor couple seen in one of the viewing booths.

Madonna established another favourite theme, that of the Spanish dancer, with her next promotional film, for 'La Isla Bonita' in March 1987. It also incorporates a religious strand as her character, in an elongated vest that could double as a slip and a dress, fingers a string of rosary beads and a crucifix and stares from beneath her slicked-back, mousey hair at a band playing out in the street, imagining herself to be a fabulous dancer in a stunning red flamenco dress.

Life imitated art, again, when the Latin look turned up in the shops in the guise of boleros and layered skirts.

Madonna's womanly curves were firmer, more streamlined these days. She was already in "great physical condition" when she attended aerobics classes at Hollywood health centre The Sports Connection before her marriage to Sean, according to its manager John McCormick. At the club, the arrogant behaviour of "The Material Bitch", as she was nicknamed, did not endear her to the clientele.

By the summer, when she went out on her *Who's That Girl?* world tour, she would have a personal trainer, and her daily routine would include jogging, weight-lifting, dancing, gymnastics, trampolining, swimming or cycling. Always, she ate vegetarian food with plenty of protein and carbohydrate, and avoided the sun.

Seen off-duty, she would usually be kitted out in running pants, trainers, T-shirt, baseball cap and sunglasses.

The tour was one part of a project which also involved a film, the flop *Who's That Girl?*, and its soundtrack album. Co-

starring with Griffin Dunne, Coati Mundi and a live cougar, Madonna and director Jamie Foley had high hopes for the slapstick comedy, in which Madonna played a jailbird called Nikki Finn, drawing from both Monroe and actress Judy Holliday, and wore a variety of tutus and ra-ra skirts over her fishnets. The American public was apathetic, and the press scathing.

The tour, however, was a massive success. Closely involved in every aspect of the planning, Madonna took to the road, supported by British funk band Level 42, with a full-scale extravaganza that included three backing singers, a team of male dancers and a succession of quickfire costume changes.

Madonna's blonde hair was growing longer, and its soft curls made for a striking contrast with the firm, almost hard lines of her eye make-up and lipstick, presided over by her friend Debi M.

Collaborating with Marlene Stewart on the clothes, Madonna expanded on the idea of bringing her popular video characters to life onstage, reworking scenes from 'True Blue', 'Papa Don't Preach', 'La Isla Bonita', where she wore a flouncy, beaded, Spanish-style dress, and 'Open Your Heart'. This was performed in Marlene's memorable, black ensemble with its tassels, golden tips and ribbing, and fishnets, while thirteen-year-old Chris Finch acted out the boy's role. A gold lamé jacket doubled for 'White Heat''s gangland and a rendition of 'Causing A Commotion'.

In case anyone should have taken Madonna too seriously, or imagined that *she* took *herself* too seriously, the star made sure there was lashings of humour.

In an amusing take on her tradition of message clothes, she spelt out the phrase "You can dance" on a jacket using the letter U, a can of soup and the word "dance" at the back.

And she royally took the piss in the most ridiculous outfit known to mankind, coming on like a grotesque Dame Edna Everage with a hat strewn with fake fruit, flowers and feathers, jewelled batwing spectacles with heavy, black frames, a red, ruffled skirt and a bodice completely covered with objects – everything from dolls to watches. Oh, and fishnets. And knickers inscribed at the back with the word KISS. Unusually for Madonna, it was all more ludicrous than humorous, but thus clad, she sang 'Dress You Up', 'Material Girl' and 'Like A Virgin'.

The tour was memorable for Madonna in more ways than one. In Torino, she enjoyed a meeting with her Italian cousin, Amelia, and her family. Her great-aunt Bambina said of Madonna: "In my times we didn't behave like that." But despite wanting to embrace her famous relative, the ailing Bambina couldn't make it to Torino.

The Dancer's Story

Chris Finch was just thirteen when he was plucked from obscurity to dance with Madonna on her "Who's That Girl?" tour in 1987. He had turned up to audition for the boy's role that Madonna had created in the video for 'Open Your Heart'. Bringing the storyline to the stage, she needed a young dancer to sneak into her peepshow.

At the time, Chris's friends were all ardent Madonna admirers. He was a more recent convert, who had seen the light with the release of *True Blue*. But when Chris, from Anaheim, California, began working with Madonna, he became "her biggest fan" and still is.

Asked what was so special about her, the man who kissed Madonna every night for months, onstage, explains: "As a person, there is something that sets her apart from everybody else. I was with her every day on the tour. My hotel suite was next to hers. We had a special connection. She was very nice – it was like we were old friends right away. Madonna wanted to keep everything as sane as possible for me."

To this end, she arranged that his mother and a tutor travelled with him on tour. But the lessons he learnt from Madonna were among the most valuable of his life. "Madonna and Sean Penn were like surrogate parents. They both went out of their way for me. She was like a second mum. I learnt more from her than I ever did in school. She told me to do things that make you happiest. Not only that – if you do something, do it a hundred per cent. Don't do anything half-assed. And you know what, it has made me a better performer."

Chris is quick to defend Madonna against allegations made in books about her behaviour on that tour. "I read recently that Madonna was supposedly a holy terror, that she wouldn't talk to the crew or dancers and that we weren't allowed to look at her offstage. Let me tell you, that is so untrue. It's all lies. She's not like that at all. She had no diva moments. Madonna talked to everybody, she was friends with everybody. It was sort of like having a second family."

Chris' dancing and ability to learn the routines quickly so impressed Madonna that she invited him to dance to other songs too. But 'Open Your Heart' is a special memory, especially since it was the first number. Chris therefore opened the show as the determined youngster trying to find a way into the peepshow. He recalls: "To be the first person to step up onstage in front of 65,000 people

"...her best movements are not when she's onstage but when she cuts loose on the dancefloor"

and hear the screams was electric. It was better than sex. It was better than drugs. I also had a lot of fun with 'Into The Groove' and 'Holiday'."

As a token of her appreciation, Madonna presented Chris with the famous bustier she wore for 'Like A Virgin'. "It's pretty crazy," he laughs. "It's got googly eyes for nipples."

But of all the stage clothes Madonna paraded on the tour, Chris' favourite is the legendary 'Open Your Heart' black bustier with the pointy cups, gold tips and tassels. He also fondly remembers the red, sequinned, halter bustier and pants combination that she wore for 'Holiday'. "She has a beautiful body," declares Chris, who was once with Penn when he bought a leopard-print bra and pantie set for Madonna. "You could put anything on her and she would look great."

He says of her world conquest: "She's got a lot of determination. She's a perfectionist. She's on top of her game. She gives a hundred and thirty five per cent, and she expects everyone else to give that too. She's a hell of a performer, on or off the stage – her best movements are not when she's onstage but when she cuts loose on the dancefloor.

"Any kind of group can enjoy her music. And she's bigger than life. The controversy she creates... her life has been like a good TV show. Everybody just wants to tune into it."

Chris went on to dance in the movie *I'll Do Anything* but retired from dancing at only sixteen, claiming, "It was something that I never planned to do. I just fell into it."

Still only in his late twenties, he is now associate producer of the *Rick Dees Morning Show*, the Number One-rated Top Forty radio show in the world. He's also been acting in Shakespearian productions at the LA Theatre Centre, and he is writing and singing for a solo musical project.

Chris Finch was an integral part of routines including 'Open Your Heart', 'Like A Virgin' and 'Holiday' on the Who's That Girl World Tour (opposite). The tour's theatrical routines set the standard that would later develop into the slick choreography of 1990's Blond Ambition Tour (below), showcasing Madonna's innate love of dance. Madonna whips up a frenzy (above) at the 1989 LA APLA Danceathon.

Madonna's stage persona for the Who's That Girl Tour was shaped by costumes that took their inspiration from American and Hispanic culture, as well as an outfit that would look more at home on Dame Edna Everage.

IRL ?WH

Coming on like a grotesque Dame Edna Everage with a hat strewn with fake fruit, flowers and feathers, jewelled batwing spectacles with heavy, black frames, a red, ruffled skirt and a bodice completely covered with objects

O'S THAT

T GIRL ?W

The Who's That Girl Tour
also afforded an early glimpse
of Madonna in a pointed bra,
though at this stage the tasselled
cones on her corset were more
flirtatious than threatening.
She had followed a strict work-out
routine before embarking on the
sell-out tour and was delighted to
show off her new, toned physique.

The Who's That Girl Tour played to an estimated two million concert-goers on three continents, exciting such attention that when the first Japanese show was cancelled thanks to a storm, troops were called in to control 28,000 rioting fans.

"He's the coolest guy in the universe"

Bustiers, basques, brassieres, bodies, fishnet and flesh... with the concept of underwear as outerwear catching on internationally, and young women finally free from the constraints of having to wear a white bra under a white top and never letting the straps show, Madonna had become a fashion leader, a sex goddess, a glamour queen and a Monroe for the modern girl, albeit one somewhat lacking in the fragility of Marilyn, whom she acknowledges as a "victim".

With the Number One *True Blue* album selling in its millions across the globe, lauded by the critics for its artistry, strength and variety, with homes in New York and LA and with a husband she described in her album dedication as "the coolest guy in the universe", it looked like the material girl really had it all.

But 1987 saw a deterioration in her relationship with Sean Penn. His violent tantrums, usually triggered by press intrusion and a fierce possessiveness of his flirtatious wife, had been a continuing problem in the marriage since the hostilities of *Shanghai Surprise*. The couple were having loud and very public rows.

Madonna was someone who understood and manipulated the media. She had been known to alert the papers to her comings and goings, she was quick to take advantage of a good photo opportunity, and she had posed in glamorous gowns for esteemed magazines such as Vogue and *Vanity Fair*. There were even whispers that she had secretly enjoyed the chaos of the wedding.

Sean, on the other hand, fought for his privacy ever more jealously, something Madonna described with great understatement as "not fun". In June 1987, he was sent to prison after violating his probation by punching an extra with a camera on the Colors film set and driving while over the limit. He served just over a month.

The couple were apart for much of 1988, with Sean in California and Madonna in New York where she opened in David Mamet's stage play, *Speed The Plow*, in May at the Royale Theatre, wearing a demure suit and with her hair again coloured reddish-brown. "I pursued it like a motherfucker," said Madonna of her single-minded campaign for the part.

It didn't do a lot for her reputation as an actress, and she came to find the role depressing, but Madonna's run sold out on the strength of her name alone. The press, meanwhile, were turning their attention to other matters, her rumoured romances with John Kennedy Jr (whose mother, Jackie, allegedly scuppered the relationship), veteran film star Warren Beatty, model-turned-singer Nick Kamen and, controversially, bisexual comedienne Sandra Bernhard.

Madonna, Bernhard and actress Jennifer Grey, dubbed the "Snatch Batch", reputedly caroused around lesbian bars in net tops, crop-tops, spangly bras and flowery-painted jeans, with Madonna and Sandra delighting in their frequent displays of intimacy.

They made a show-stopping appearance together on David Letterman's famous TV show, dressed identically in cut-off jeans, white T-shirts and ankle socks and black shoes. Millions of viewers watched as they bellowed with laughter, lolling butchly on the furniture, legs apart, with Sandra claiming to have bedded both Madonna and Penn.

Madonna and Sandra have since denied that they were anything more than friends. But whatever the truth, Madonna had always enjoyed gay culture and the shock value of her flirtations with lesbianism, it suited her to give the impression of a sexual liaison with Bernhard, and it infuriated Sean Penn. By now, his wife had decided they should call it a day.

On December 28, he burst into their Malibu home and, according to the newspapers, tied Madonna to a chair, terrorized her and left her there, helpless, for hours, before returning to abuse her again.

She began the new year of 1989 by filing for a divorce, leaving some to suggest that the hard-drinking Penn had served his purpose as Madonna's stepping stone into the movies.

Madonna's relationship with Sean Penn was clearly under strain from paparazzi attention by 1988, violent scenes between Penn and the press (below left) becoming commonplace. The situation wasn't helped by Madonna's public flirtation with bisexual comedienne Sandra Bernhard, seen here (below) with Madonna at the Don't Bungle The Jungle charity event at Brooklyn Academy Of Music in June '89. The duo sang 'I Got You Babe', before telling the audience to believe the rumours.

Her Collaborators

Alek Keshishian, (right) video director, filmed *In Bed With Madonna*: "With Madonna, there's nothing that's going to cancel her day. She has the same discipline whether she's well or unwell. Whether she's had a disastrous phone call or the worst night, she is at yoga every morning. There is almost no self-destructiveness in this woman."

Björk, (left) singer and co-writer of 'Bedtime Story': "In a way it was more like a little present from me to Nellee (co-writer/producer) even though I respect Madonna. Probably she's one of the persons I respect most in the world, and if there was someone I'd want to give a little present to, she'd probably be one of them...

"In the daily life, it seems as if she isn't aware of her subconscious, as silly as it may sound. I have tried to avoid her as much as I could. I like her, but she seems to be a woman obsessed with material things. The universe she surrounds herself with, I can't take it. I would much rather just bump into her in a bar by an accident not even knowing who she is."

William Orbit, co-producer, *Ray Of Light* and *Music*: "I think you could summarise Madonna as 'expect the unexpected'. She subscribes to the whole notion of keep them guessing, keep changing, keep developing. She can be very hard to work with cos her standards are so high, but easy to work with because she's so talented...

"Just as I was ready to crawl home exhausted, (she'd say), 'You can sleep when you're dead.'"

Stuart Price, Brit, musical director, keyboardist and guitarist on the "Drowned World" tour, and "teacher" of Cockney rhyming slang: "She's very sarcastic. When I'm with Americans I always assume that there's a huge humour divide. Normally if you drop in a sarcastic line, Americans look at you like you're being serious. But Madonna totally gets it...

"She's got, 'Take the third party fire and theft,' which is take a left, followed by a 'terrible fright', a right. And 'I'm in a bit of a chicken curry', hurry. I even managed to get her to admit that she is a septic. You know, a septic tank – yank."

Ricky Martin, (right) Latin pop singer, on his duet with Madonna – 'Cuidado Con Mi Corazon': "To work with Madonna, it was a beautiful experience. I mean, she affected my life, when it comes to music, in a very positive way... To be locked in a studio with her, crying a little, y'know, creating music is something I would love to do again..."She enjoys the Latin sounds, she's energetic, I'm energetic, so let's do something!... She's doing amazing with her Spanish!"

Herb Ritts, photographer since shooting *Desperately Seeking Susan* poster: "She walked in first in her Boy Toy mode, and we ended up taking pictures right off the bat. From that moment, we just really clicked. We did this one in 1990, in this old, run-down theatre. She had just changed when this shot was taken and she was laughing, and it was terrific, because it was very her. It was an unusual afternoon because we were just creating pictures to create pictures. It wasn't like we were working, we were just enjoying ourselves."

Laura Mercier, make-up artist: "Madonna is beautiful without make-up and has the sort of magical face and bone structure models dream of.

"I originally didn't want to work with her, because I felt she was far too egotistical, but after she asked me three times I agreed, and found her intelligent, organised and professional. Of course, she needs a lot of attention, but part of the job is to make her feel good. She respects what I do. She can abuse me to a certain point, because I let her, if she's feeling low or is in a bad mood. But she knows there's a limit she cannot pass, and she never does."

Donna DeLory, solo artist and Madonna backing singer since the "Blond Ambition" tour: "I love being part of something so dramatic and theatrical with Madonna. It's fun to put on another costume and be someone different... Her input to me has always been more of her sharing her own experiences as an artist and a woman so I could learn from them."

Niki Haris, (far left, with Donna DeLory) backing vocalist: "She's amazing, she's a genius, she's nuts, she's difficult. She's a mother, she's in love, she's insecure... all those things we are, but it's magnified because she's got a spotlight on her...

"Once onstage, we were singing 'La Isla Bonita' and I look down, and this one girl had her boobs hanging over the barrier. They were huge, pendulous boobs. I'm like, 'Why is she showing Madonna her boobs?' But most fans are really respectful."

Mirwais, co-producer: "It's surprising to find myself working with the most famous artist in the world. But in the studio you forget it. She's a simple, normal, sociable person with a really good sense of humour."

DJ Richard "Humpty" Vission, remixer: "She could have just done a pop record. This album (*Music*) is testament that she's still on top of her shit."

Jamie King, "Drowned World" tour director and choreographer: "Madonna wants what she always wants... *edgy*."

Monte Pittman, guitarist and guitar tutor for Madonna: "I don't see how she ever sleeps, because whatever she does, it seems like she spends a lot of time practising."

Michael Rosenblatt, former Sire executive: "I find it ridiculous when people accuse Madonna of selling sex. Sex and rock'n'roll fit together so perfectly that everyone in this business sells sex."

The Prodigy, one of Maverick's first signings: "Madonna herself did a great deal to woo the Prodigy to the label. She was very, very clued up about the band and the British dance scene."

Camille Barbone, former manager: "She could put on horrible clothes and pull it off. She'd buy a shirt for fifty cents and cut it. She usually wore oversized clothes. Her hair was all ratted."

Christopher Flynn, first dance teacher: "Madonna was one of the best students I ever had... A lot of men have complained that Madonna used them and then discarded them, bit I think that's just sour grapes. I didn't feel the slightest bit exploited."

"It dealt with a *lot* of taboos *and it made* people *afraid...* *I think it had* a lot of *positive* messages"

There were similar sneers of "career move" about her next romance with Warren Beatty, a man whose friends and contacts featured highly on the Tinseltown A-list. While they discussed plans for the film *Dick Tracy*, another worldwide outrage was about to hit the fan.

As Madonna prepared to release her new album and its title track as a single, she signed a multi-million dollar deal with Pepsi. She would film a series of ads, with the first including an exclusive extract from 'Like A Prayer', and Pepsi would pay her for the endorsement and also sponsor her next tour.

The ad – a sentimental scenario in which the child Madonna meets her older, successful self – aired as planned. But when MTV screened Madonna's own video for the song, there was a huge hullabaloo. Amid screams of "Blasphemy!" from religious and moral organisations, a statement of disapproval from the Vatican and mounting pressure on Pepsi to drop their star, the company did just that. Madonna kept the money – and the prestige.

The 'Like A Prayer' video proved too hot to handle for Pepsi, who dropped out of their sponsorship of her forthcoming tour and pulled the commercial which was shown only once, on March 2, 1989. Madonna probably wasn't too concerned, having pocketed a cool $5 million for the ad.

The video, directed by Mary Lambert, contains the strongest, most atmospheric scenes Madonna has ever filmed in its exploration of religious and sexual ecstasy – a link that had preoccupied the singer since her church-going days as a child.

It also delivers an anti-racist statement, with Madonna, clad in a slip, her hair shoulder-length, dark and fluffy, making love in church to a black man – a saint's statue come to life. In other moments, Madonna develops stigmata, she joins in the joyous performance of a black gospel choir, she witnesses a murder and she sings in front of blazing crucifixes.

With its contrastingly dark and delirious atmospheres, it remains Madonna's most powerful video. "It dealt with a lot of taboos," said Madonna. "And it made people afraid... I think it had a lot of positive messages." She told the *New York Times*: "The theme of Catholicism runs rampant through my album. It's me struggling with the mystery and magic that surrounds it."

'Like A Prayer' was again co-produced by Madonna, Steve Bray and Patrick Leonard, and the tracks were written and co-written by Madonna – including a collaboration with Prince, who completed his part of the 'Love Song' duet by post.

There was great critical acclaim for the musical imagination of the album, which took several steps back from the dancefloor to absorb some new shades of colour and emotion and the odd black influence from the music of Madonna's youth.

This was a much more personal affair than anything Madonna had yet released. Dedicated to "my mother, who taught me how to pray", it confronted childhood issues involving her family, as well as her unhappy marriage, and the video for 'Oh Father' is harrowingly autobiographical.

At the time released only in America, it recreates the death scene of a young mother and explores the tempestuous relationship that ensues between the husband and daughter she has left behind. Madonna, as the grown daughter, all blonde tips on short, dark, bushy hair, is reconciled with the father as they meet years later at the grave – but not before history repeats itself when she falls in love with an equally tyrannical suitor. Typically, Madonna delivers an ambiguity in the word "father" – "Oh, Father, I have sinned... "

She later described the video as "an attempt to embrace and accept my mother's death".

"If you *don't* say what you want, *then you're* not going to *get* it"

Elsewhere, the roleplay arising from this phase of her career is less brooding. Especially extravagant is the promo clip for 'Express Yourself', in which Madonna – who oversaw every aspect of the project – acts out scenes of status, power and desire, before finally asserting control over her own life and body.

In a setting inspired by the Twenties film *Metropolis*, much of the action takes place underground where men are working manually, sweating like slaves, while an idle Madonna passes her days in a rich apartment. Inevitably the two worlds collide – and each has something to offer the other.

Madonna introduces a new accessory – a monocle swinging round her neck – in the course of the video, where she acts out two visions of women: the naked one wearing the collar and chain, the black corset and suspenders, and the masculine, crotch-grabbing power-dame in the dark blue, baggy trouser suit, flashing a glimpse of bra and smoking a cigarette.

Madonna starts out in a lime-green, sleeveless dress, her hair in a short, blonde, wavy bob, parted to the side, and ends up crawling along the floor to lick a saucer like a big cat on the prowl – a more dangerous version of the small, black moggie she has been stroking earlier in the video. As a cat, Madonna pours the milk over her shoulder, suggestively, before a rippling hunk, who has rescued her pet from the wet underground, arrives with the animal and claims his reward . . .

The final, written message states: "Without the heart there can be no understanding between the hand and the mind."

Madonna herself has stated: "The ultimate thing behind the song is that if you don't express yourself, if you don't say what you want, then you're not going to get it. And in effect you are chained down by your inability to say what you feel or go after what you want."

Less busy, less serious, is the video for 'Cherish', in which Madonna looks as fresh and delightful as the song itself sounds. Returning to the feathery, blonde, waif look of 'Papa Don't Preach', with minimum make-up and a simple, black, mini-dress buttoned at the front, she romps in the sea with mermen and reveals maternal instincts with some tender scenes involving a boy merchild.

There's no such innocence about the album's artwork, but there is a humour at work in the cover shot which harks back to The Rolling Stones' *Sticky Fingers* sleeve of the early Seventies. By comparison with the rockers' famous denim crotch and zip, the photo zooms in on Madonna's lower stomach, belly-button and hips, where the top button of her jeans is unfastened.

She springs a surprise on both this and the back cover picture with a return to her jewellery box. Her fingers are encircled by rings, her waist gleams with strings of beads and baubles, and that old favourite, the crucifix, is reinstated around her neck.

In stark contrast to the homely brunette of 'Like A Prayer', Madonna's image in 'Express Yourself' was harshly ambiguous, blonde and stylised. The star alternately paraded in a double-breasted suit with monocle and writhed naked, chained to a bed before seducing British male model Cameron. Feminists were outraged.

"A tough outer shell at times protects hidden vulnerability"

Jean Paul Gaultier

The Blond Ambition tour was notorious for its theatrical presentation and awe-inspiring choreography. Few costumes are as firmly embedded in public consciousness as the Gaultier-designed gold corset paraded in 'Like A Virgin' (opposite). Accompanied by two male dancers dressed as pointy-breasted eunuchs. Madonna fondled herself to the strains of Eastern music during a routine that nearly got her arrested in Toronto.

Sado-masochism and masturbation were just a couple of the themes that made the "Blond Ambition" tour in the spring and summer of 1990 such a hot ticket.

No longer having to worry about Sean Penn's disapproval, Madonna plunged full-tilt into a world of outrageous sexual fantasy, colluding with Marlene Stewart but mostly with over-the-top fashion designer Jean Paul Gaultier to create an extravaganza of erotica and exotica, velvet and satin, complete with breastplates, conical bras and corsetry. It was a brilliant partnership.

Gaultier, who had long specialised in such garments, explained, "The inspiration is from me and her, but first of all, it's from her," and he said of his bullet bra designs: "A tough outer shell at times protects hidden vulnerability."

Madonna recalled: "I sent him drawings originally of what I wanted. A lot of costumes were inspired by my stick drawings – I'm not a good artist – and then he threw his stuff in."

These outfits would take on a huge, symbolic importance, representing everything Madonna stood for at this point in her career. She was simply saying, "Do your own thing. Don't worry about what's expected, or what everyone else is doing."

In these encouragements of sexual liberation, Madonna played with the roles of the sexes, blurred the genders, explored the male and female in every person and, in Gaultier's most extreme creations, permitted herself a chuckle at men and their fantasies about women.

A section of the show was set in a church where Madonna, shamed, guilty and candlelit in a black cloak with a hood and a large gold crucifix, sang below a stained-glass window while a "priest" swung incense.

The show began with 'Express Yourself', in a stage set recreating the underground/overground environment of the video, with a troupe of male dancers playing the working men. Madonna made her entrance with her hair stretched tautly back into a topknot and long, fake, blonde ponytail, a style which was replaced for the European dates by a short, peroxide tangle.

Her make-up was extremely severe, the brows thickly blackened and the eyelids gleaming with colour and a heavy application of dark liner.

Her outfit made for a perfect visual combination of masculine and feminine: a double-breasted suit with a difference, a mix of equally prominent underwear and outerwear. The tight jacket was cut with slits, allowing the bra cones to point through. Even more dramatically, Madonna was wearing her pink bodysuit and suspenders over the baggy trousers. A finishing touch was her favourite new accessory, the monocle chain.

Minus the jacket for 'Open Your Heart', Madonna showed off the imposing, satin bodysuit in all its warrioresque finery – the quilted, pointy cones, the boning and the straps, which replicated all the detail of a vintage corset. She was in

perfect shape to show off her body, working out with her trainer for up to three hours a day.

Eager to establish her physical and emotional superiority to men, the dominatrix Madonna quickly humped one of the dancers before carrying on with an exhibitionistic dance routine, using the familiar chair as her prop. She asserted her dominance over women, too, in the wrestling scene created for 'Causing A Commotion'.

However, it was her performance on a red, velvet bed that raised protests from parents and moral crusaders around the world. She was flanked on either side by male dancers clad in black slave headwear and gold, velvet, ridiculously prominent bras, which they fondled suggestively as she rolled around, simulating masturbation. Dressed in a shiny gold top with the trademark cones and matching knickers, plus her fishnets, Madonna frantically thrust her groin into the sheets and pillows as she worked her way to the climax of an Egyptian-flavoured reading of 'Like A Virgin'. Clearly, she needed the confession that followed.

In another part of the show, she appeared as Breathless Mahoney, her character from *Dick Tracy*, sitting on a black grand piano in a beautifully tailored, black tail-jacket and a sparkling, emerald-green body suit with the usual torpedo cups.

With 'Hanky Panky', the spanking song, offering the opportunity for a crack or two about smacking bottoms and 'Now I'm Following You' culminating in a display by a line of dancers dressed as Dick Tracy in yellow raincoats and fedoras, Madonna and her backing singers followed on with a bit of light relief, taking the stage in dressing gowns and hair rollers. Later, they would indulge in a little vulgar girl-talk, while Madonna, a committed safe-sex campaigner, made it her business to extol the joys of condoms.

The 'Cherish' video came to life with the appearance of three dancing mermen, and the softest costume of the show was Marlene's black mini-dress trimmed with down from a West African stork, the marabou. It was like Christmas had come. Finally, Madonna, a vision of black and flesh in a longline bra with terrifying cups, belted cycle shorts and a strip of netting round her middle, danced through 'Vogue' with her troupe.

Returning for an encore of 'Holiday', Madonna sported the much-photographed polka-dot outfit – a short, spotty bolero with matching flounces at the bottoms of white trousers – and closed the evening with 'Family Affair' and 'Keep It Together' in an all-black ensemble involving a cage vest, the longline bra, skintight shorts, kneepads and a bowler hat, another nod to Liza Minnelli in *Cabaret*.

Magazines all over splashed Madonna on their cover. She was pictured in her tour costumes in everything from *Harper's Bazaar* to *Lui*, *Photo* to *The Face*.

Elle, in a feature about the revival of bondage gear, proposed that such items now represented personal choice and sexual freedom rather than their earlier statements of

BLOND

Apart from the conical bra, another Blond Ambition hallmark was the *I Dream Of Jeannie* ponytail worn throughout Japan and the States. By the time the tour reached Europe, the hairpiece was dropped, as it was damaging Madonna's follicles.

AMBITIO

Gaultier's sleek and figure-flattering designs were an ideal complement for Madonna's frenetic dance routines. She wore a combination of babydoll dress and cycling shorts for 'Into The Groove' and 'Cherish' (above left), while a polka-dotted clown outfit adapted from a *My Fair Lady* costume was perfect for 'Holiday' (above right). For 'Hanky Panky' and 'Now I'm Following You' (left), she stripped off a sheer black gown to reveal this glittering green and white fringed corset.

NBLOND

AMBITIO

n't worry about what's
one else is doing

N

WhatMadonnaSaysAboutThem...

On The Gaultier Bra

Madonna to Norman Mailer on her Gaultier cone bras

"There's something kind of medieval and interesting about them.

I asked Gaultier to do the costumes for my ("Blond Ambition") tour, and he already had these designs in one of his collections, but now I (also) had two male dancers coming out in them.

It's very camp.

Women used to wear those cones on their heads, but now they've become like a bra.

The idea is to take something meant for one part of the body and place it on another part.

Also, they're pointed. So there's something slightly dangerous about them. If you bump into them, you'll cut yourself ...

"The idea behind it is that breasts are these soft things that men rely on to some extent, so it's a way of saying, 'Fuck off'. Just think of my breasts in another way, that's all, not something soft you can fall into.

Believe me, I love to have my breasts touched by a man that I care for, but it's really important to me that people look at life a different way, seeing that women can seduce and women can have sexual fantasies.

"Plus the idea that the men were wearing them. I was singing 'Like A Virgin' lying on this red, velvet bed, and I reversed the whole Playboy Bunny thing, just two Playboy Bunnies in some costume that pushes their bodies into some unnatural shape, but now it's the men.

I was having an inverted fantasy of that in my show... Just another way of getting people to look at it...

"I've been accused for years and years, especially at the beginning of my career, of setting the women's movement back because I was being sexual in a traditional way, with my corsets and push-up bras and garter belts and this and that, and feminists were beating the fuck out of me: 'What are you doing? You're sending out all the wrong messages to young girls! They should be using their heads, not their tits and their asses.'

My whole thing is you use all you have, your sexuality, your femininity, any testosterone you have inside of you, your intellect – use whatever you have and use bits and pieces wherever it's good."

"The force of her fantasy is accessible for everyone from eighteen to eighty"

1990 was Madonna's year of Hollywood glamour. Inspired by her role as sultry chanteuse Breathless Mahoney in Warren Beatty's *Dick Tracy* (this page), she injected the 'Vogue' video (opposite), with the spirit of golden age Hollywood. Here she pays homage to a famous Helmut Newton photograph in a see-through top that gave MTV bosses an aneurysm.

submission. The magazine decided: "These clothes are modern armour – it's a look that is as threatening as it is alluring. Moreover, it's about autoeroticism."

Vogue declared that, "The force of her fantasy is accessible for everyone from eighteen to eighty." The fantasy may have been accessible enough, but few senior citizens were reported to be wearing basques at the bingo hall. Madonna was simply too much for some cities on the "Blond Ambition" tour, refusing to tone down the "immoral" masturbation scenes in response to police appeals in Toronto. After seeing the show, the officers decided not to proceed with charges of "lewd" and "obscene" behaviour.

Madonna also suffered disappointing ticket sales in Rome and was forced to cancel two Italian concerts after churchmen declared her sacrilegious. She called a press conference in which she memorably challenged her accusers: "If you are sure I'm a sinner, then let he who has not sinned cast the first stone."

The tour, she said, was a reflection of "light and dark, joy and sorrow, redemption and salvation". Furthermore, it was "a celebration of love, life and humanity".

One of the most satisfying aspects of the tour for Madonna was the interest she drummed up in the film, *Dick Tracy*. Her 'Vogue' single was included on Madonna's soundtrack album, *I'm Breathless*, although not in the film. It had already been a monster hit in March, launching a new and amusing dance craze which Madonna had appropriated from the gay, black, male habitués of cool New York clubland.

"Strike the pose!" The essence of Vogueing was to adopt the stance and mannerisms of a catwalk model or film star while dancing, using lots of haughty stares and arm and hand movements. In Madonna's video demonstration, appropriately filmed in black and white, she reels off a list of inspirational actors and actresses, the ones she had adored in her childhood.

Praising the Hollywood idols for their style and grace, and hilariously proclaiming that Rita Hayworth "gave good face", Madonna appears in white-blonde curls dressed this way and that to look retro, and later concealed by a long wig. With costumes including white and black gowns, a lace-up corset and a suit with the jacket hanging open to reveal her underwear, she also boasts a heaving cleavage under a see-through lace top and, unforgettably, points her best bra forward – a Gaultier, of course.

The album, *I'm Breathless*, was co-written by Madonna, Pat Leonard, Broadway composer Stephen Sondheim and singer/songwriter Andy Paley with the brief that the songs must sound contemporary yet in tune with the music of the Thirties. It was released in May to rave reviews and a Number Two chart position – although more gratifying to Madonna must have been the praise and acceptance she received for her role as a nightclub singer in the film. It was a long time coming. Madonna had been trying in vain since *Desperately Seeking Susan* to become a credible actress.

A tremendous box office success when it hit the cinemas in June, acclaimed as much for its style and colour as its humorous storyline, *Dick Tracy* portrayed a multi-faceted Madonna: gorgeous and witty, sharp and sexual. She had worked hard to redevelop her busty curves after years of gruelling work-out sessions that had made her body strong and toned but not traditionally womanly. Now, she was showing off an impressive cleavage in the beautiful, low-cut, clinging gowns she wore as Breathless Mahoney – although there was no gain without pain. Madonna later complained that she spent more time having costumes fitted than she did actually filming, and some of the creations squeezed her mercilessly.

Little wonder that she attended the Washington premiere in a loose, dark, strappy dress, so low-slung around the breasts that they looked like they were hitting her waist. Sunglasses, clumpy shoes and a crucifix completed the casual, summery look.

Contrastingly, the outfit she wore to the seventh annual MTV Awards in September was the most extravagant of her career. Enthused by the popularity of *Dangerous Liaisons*, Madonna borrowed one of the period costumes from the film to perform 'Vogue' as Marie Antoinette, with her dancers/courtiers also authentically kitted out in ruffled shirts, waistcoats, frock-coats – and shorts!

Her cramped bosoms rose above a tight-fitting bodice, folds of patterned skirt fell from wide hoops to billow round her legs, her wig defied gravity, and she sealed the effect with a choker made from strings of pearls, a fan, a pair of opera glasses and a perfectly observed make-up job, the face ghostly white and a beauty spot painted in below the eye.

It was a saucy and funny performance, Madonna undermining her regal stature by flashing her passion-killers at the audience, and encouraging her courtiers to grope her and peep under the voluminous folds of her dress.

'Vogue' was good too.

VOGUE

Invoking the spirits of Jean Harlow and Marlene Dietrich, Madonna's unique vision owed much to the work of Thirties photographers Horst and Hurrell, but was inevitably stamped with her own exquisitely glamorous personality.

GO

ODFACE

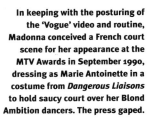

In keeping with the posturing of the 'Vogue' video and routine, Madonna conceived a French court scene for her appearance at the MTV Awards in September 1990, dressing as Marie Antoinette in a costume from *Dangerous Liaisons* to hold saucy court over her Blond Ambition dancers. The press gaped.

WhatTheySayAboutMadonna...

Hopelessly Devoted

While many of today's contemporary artists acknowledge their Madonna influence, some of the most unlikely musicians take their respect one step beyond.

TOBY MORSE, singer of New York's melodic hardcore punk band H20, has a five-inch tattoo on his forearm of the image on Madonna's *True Blue* album sleeve, and the group have covered 'Like A Prayer' – albeit "a lot faster with heavier breakdowns, but with H20's sense of melody."

So, Toby, what's all this about?

"I grew up on punk rock music, but I've always loved Madonna. She doesn't give a fuck what anybody thinks. She does what she wants. I got the tattoo because *True Blue* is a great album. She was still young and hungry for success. 'Papa Don't Preach' – come on, that's a classic. But I like every era of Madonna. They each had their own style statement and sexiness.

"I've met her twice. The first time was at CBGBs at a pre-Lollapalooza party. I was there with all my friends: it was our hang-out. She was with one dude – Guy Oseary. I walked up to her and showed her my tattoo. She looked a little nervous because she had no bodyguards, but she took my arm and said she was flattered. I got an autograph from her, and it was so surreal to me.

"A year and a half later, my friends Rancid were playing at the Roseland in NYC and she was up there trying to sign them to her label. I was introduced to her again by them and she said she remembered me and pointed out to her friends that I had a tattoo of her. Even more surreal.

"She'll be remembered for her individuality, open sexuality, creativity, smart business sense, the longevity of her career – and she never got boring!"

MIKE WATT, founder of San Pedro's pioneering Eighties hardcore band the Minutemen, has formed an occasional tribute group called The Madonnabes. Mike, now playing bass in fIREHOSE, also teamed up with Sonic Youth to form the offshoot band Ciccone Youth. Their first release was a three-track Madonna-tribute single in 1987 comprising 'Burnin' Up', 'Tuff Titty Rap' and 'Into The Groove(y)'.

Mike talks about Madonna: "She's a real inspiration – never manipulated but always in control. I was turned on to her in the middle Eighties by Kira, who was playing bass in Black Flag at the time. Symbolically, Madonna represents to me the power women can have through music and, through that, what anyone can make possible when they can be empowered. A pretty punk rock idea in a lot of ways: power for the disenfranchised, the outsider who can't fit in but still has something to say and ideas to create from.

"When d. boon (Minutemen founder) was killed, she became even more of an important inspiration for me. I was shaken tremendously by him passing and wanted to quit music all together. Madonna helped me stick with it. That might sound crazy coming from a forty-three-year-old punk rocker, but it's the truth.

"The Madonnabes usually do about forty-five minutes, twelve tunes. These are not just bar-band Top Forty covers of her songs. I work a very present and muscular bass guitar and try to emphasize my musical personality as seen through her works. Some people find it crazy that I have anything to do with her, and I like that aspect of blowing their minds. That's why I used to wear a mouse suit when I played with The Madonnabes live. They were not my tunes, and I want to acknowledge the fact that I was 'sidemousing' her material – not just an out-and-out copy but an interpretation via a weird punk rocker from San Pedro.

"With Ciccone Youth, Thurston (Moore) picked the name. Kim Gordon and Thurston were always big Madonna fans. I think they liked the way she was fucking with culture in the Eighties. I was with Thurston in their apartment and I said to him, 'You know, I want to make a single where I interpret a Madonna tune. Will you guys do one too and we'll make a forty-five?' I did 'Burning Up' and Thurston picked 'Into The Groove' and wrote an intro rap for it, the 'Tuff Titty Rap'.

"Madonna has been an inspiration to me in tons of ways, from the way I work my bass to how I write my music and lyrics. It might not appear that way, but the sexuality she imbues fires up my playing big time. She'll be remembered for her dedication and constant drive, her ability to face down fear and overcome.

Mike Watt, founder of hardcore band The Minutemen, regularly covers Madonna songs, proving that her influence isn't restricted to mainstream parameters.

"If I met her, I'd say, 'Thank you for being yourself and being such an inspiration. Thank you for the confidence you instilled in me to do my best and not be afraid.'"

JUSTIFY JUSTIFY
JUSTIFY JUSTIFY

JUSTIFY
JUSTIFY

"She doesn't want to *live* off *camera*"

Madonna pushed the sexual angle to new and giddy limits at the end of 1990. The video for 'Justify My Love' ventured right up to the edge of hard core with its scenes of uninhibited carnal activity, in the middle of which Madonna shares an open-mouthed, lesbian kiss.

MTV refused point-blank to screen it, leaving Madonna to enjoy the storms of publicity and the kudos of releasing the first-ever video single – her answer to the ban. Madonna's co-star was her post-Beatty boyfriend Tony Ward, a model and hopeful actor in his twenties.

Directed by Jean Baptiste Mondino, who was responsible for 'Open Your Heart' – her first aggressively sexual video – the clip reveals Madonna, with brightly blonde, dishevelled hair and the black brows of the "Blond Ambition" tour, in various states of undress in a Paris hotel room. As she romps with her lovers on the bed – first Tony Ward, then, as he looks on, the butch woman whom she kisses – she flicks in and out of the black and white footage in combinations of glamorous black lingerie. Around her a veritable orgy is in progress. Men look like women, women look like men, androgynes look like either, gay men embrace, women paint on moustaches, and everywhere people writhe and fondle themselves and each other.

Clearly, this was another representation of Madonna's contention that anything goes between consenting men and women, gays and straights, and that things don't always have to be what they seem or what society deems they should be. It also gave Madonna a return trip to the on-off romance with lesbianism which had won her so much attention in the past. MTV just thought it was porn.

The song, a series of erotic murmurs carried along on sleepy rhythms, was written mostly by Lenny Kravitz with some help on the lyrics from Madonna. It was originally conceived,

along with 'Rescue Me', as one of two new songs to be included in a CD and video hits package called *The Immaculate Collection*, which was being produced for the Christmas market.

Madonna claimed to be outraged at MTV's rejection of the video: "Why is it that people are willing to go to a movie and watch someone get blown to bits for no reason, and nobody wants to see two girls kissing or two men snuggling?" The result of the controversy was to sweep 'Justify My Love' and *The Immaculate Collection* straight to the top of the CD and video charts.

By then, it was rumoured that Madonna had experienced cosmetic treatment for the first time, having collagen injections to her lips to make them thicker. Although it was not believed that she repeated the experiment, the *Justify My Love* video cover portrait was seized upon as evidence that she had tried it out, as were the "biker" photos appearing around the same time. These found her leaning forward, aggressively, in a sleeveless waistcoat with her hair scrunched up under a black cap, her face wearing a "come-on-if-you-think-you're-hard-enough" expression and a cigarette hanging out of juicy, scarlet lips. Mouth apart, it was a particularly masculine pose: Madonna, at times, could look as butch as the next man. Moreover, she could steer her appearance perilously close to drag when she overdid it with the panstick and the wigs.

Dick Tracy was still making waves, with one of the songs from the soundtrack winning an Oscar at the Academy Awards on 25 March 1991. Stephen Sondheim was not present to pick up his gong for 'Sooner Or Later', but Madonna was on hand to sing it. She swept through the back door of the Shrine Auditorium in LA with her surprise date Michael Jackson.

They made a spectacular couple; a photographer's dream. Madonna looked sensational in a low-cut, strapless

"See – *I get* what I want!"

Bob Mackie creation that clung to her curves and glittered with thousands of sequins. With a white, fluffy stole draped over her shoulders and a reported $20 million worth of diamond jewellery sparkling around her body, she wore long, white gloves and carried a beaded clutch bag. Her hair, side-parted and blonde, tumbled in waves to her shoulders, and her make-up was dramatic but not harsh, with outlined, shadowed and highlighted eyes, emphatic eyebrows and red lips. It was another touch of that Monroe magic.

During 'Sooner Or Later', Madonna performed a tease for the audience, peeling off her gloves, toying with the stole, and finally revealing the show-stopping dress. At the post-awards party, she reportedly left Jackson in the care of his disapproving friend Diana Ross to spent the rest of the night fussing over her ex-boyfriend, Warren Beatty.

It's unlikely they were discussing *In Bed With Madonna*, the warts-and-all documentary film of the "Blond Ambition" tour which was due for release in May 1991. Titled *Truth Or Dare* in America, it was a project that Beatty had warned against, due to the relentless, fly-on-the-wall filming by music video director Alek Keshishian. When Madonna insists that the cameras roll for her throat examination by a doctor, Beatty utters his famous line: "She doesn't want to *live* off camera."

In his own appearances in the film, he shrinks into the background where possible, looking uncomfortable and only just indulgent as Madonna henpecks and harangues him. For all the marriage rumours, it's hardly surprising that, a short time later, the couple were history.

Madonna is seen to treat Beatty like a sugar-daddy, receiving his gift of a Dolce and Gabbana shirt with a self-satisfied: "See – I get what I want!" And in one extraordinary scene, she is heard shouting down the phone at the legendary actor.

She shouts a lot. She shouts when she's worried, impatient or angry, when a monitor fails or her headset cuts out. And when she's shouting, she has no wish to hear the recipient's explanation. This, of course, is the backstage action that everyone wants to see, shot in black and white to contrast with the rainbow-coloured concert footage.

If Madonna's intention was to cast some warm and likeable rays over her public image, then there are scenes in which she succeeds. She brings her father onstage to lead the audience in a chorus of 'Happy Birthday' to him, and bows at his feet. In another birthday celebration, she recites a poem she has written for her personal assistant. She giggles and gossips with Sandra Bernhard. She mothers her seven male dancers, and when rumours arise in the press that she is having an affair with the only one who is heterosexual, she attempts to pacify him and smooth out the jealousies that have arisen among the others.

She dedicates her Aids benefit show in New York to her old friend, graffiti artist Keith Haring, who decorated some of her earliest clothes, including the denim jacket and a skirt in the 'Borderline' video, and she's almost inseparable from her gay brother, Christopher.

Talking about the first few "almost perfect" weeks in Europe, Madonna likens the entourage to The Partridge Family, gives her team a solemn pep talk before every show and leads them in a circle of prayer. She plays the good, rude sport in a game of truth or dare, naming Sean Penn as the love of her life and carrying out her legendary simulation of oral sex on a bottle of water. She takes her troupe shopping at Chanel. She bids farewell to the dancers at the end of the tour when they are, literally, in bed with Madonna, amid screams of laughter, mock tears and tantrums, and declarations of love.

Equally, there are scenes in which Madonna is not so much fun. Hearing her two backing vocalists singing Belinda Carlisle, she snaps: "Those girls annoy me." She makes gagging gestures behind the back of Kevin Costner, to whom she's just been chatting politely, and appears amused to learn that the tour's make-up lady has been drugged and assaulted by a stranger from a club. She lectures her father on the phone, hunched over a bowl of soup, her legs splayed and a shower cap on her head, slurping noisily as she talks. She jokes about her brother Martin's attempts to recover from alcohol abuse, and refuses to receive him when he turns up late to her hotel.

In one remarkable scene, Madonna visits her mother's grave and stretches out on the ground where she imagines her own incarceration, before jumping up suddenly and gliding off in her limo.

It makes for uncomfortable viewing, too, when Madonna fobs off her childhood friend Moira McFarland who invites her to be godmother to her forthcoming child. She also insists that Moira showed her how to insert tampons and also "finger-fucked" her, despite her friend's embarrassed protests that she can remember no such incidents.

The film does satisfy Madonna's hope that she is portrayed as the captain of the ship, pulling everyone together, although the "family" atmosphere that is stressed so strongly may be misleading: three of the dancers – including the one she was reported to have seduced – went on to sue her over the offstage footage, for which they claimed they were entitled to payment. They finally settled out of court, unable to afford any further legal action.

A particularly amusing series of events transpires after Madonna tells Sandra Bernhard that the person she most wants to meet is Spanish film star Antonio Banderas, whom she fancies. As if by magic, she later encounters Antonio in Madrid, only to discover that he's married.

"He's not such a good actor all," she huffs. "Needless to say, I never saw or heard from Antonio again."

Well, it was true at the time...

Watched by over 100 million viewers, Madonna accompanied Michael Jackson to the Oscars on March 25, 1991. She stole the show with her rendition of Stephen Sondheim's 'Sooner Or Later' (overleaf), dripping with $20 million worth of borrowed diamonds, paying tribute to Monroe and name-checking 'Stormin' Norman Schwarzkopf.

SOONER

OR LATER

The Designers

Madonna has enjoyed long associations with certain favourite designers, with Jean Paul Gaultier, Dolce & Gabbana, Versace, John Galliano and Stella McCartney, who has moved from Chloe to Gucci, springing to mind immediately. But Madonna has worn and enjoyed the clothes, footwear, make-up and jewellery of many fashionable names, and as a bonus for being a world-famous clothes-horse, no longer has to pay for her pleasures.

Among the star names claiming a place in her wardrobe are Chanel, Cartier, Prada, Bruce, Vivienne Westwood, Philip Treacy, Donna Karan, Oscar de la Renta, Gianfranco Ferrer, Balenciaga, Nike, Dior, Adidas, Fendi, Comme Des Garcons, Betsy Johnson, Stephen Sprouse, Nicolas Ghesquiere and Gucci, after its ailing fortunes had been revived by Texan Tom Ford.

Newer designers include twin brothers Dean and Dan Caten, working with a label called DSquared. They collaborated on the cowgirl section of the "Drowned World" tour, making Madonna's rodeo-style shirt, muddy jeans and suede chaps with Swarovski crystals. Catherine Malandrino, a designer working in New York, contributed a T-shirt to the tour while Michael Schmidt made a punk choker and cuffs set studded with Swarovski crystals as well as the "Fuck off" guitar strap.

Jean Paul Gaultier "The first time I saw Madonna, I was in Paris and I was looking at the TV. They were showing *Top Of The Pops*. She had a hit with 'Holiday'. I was fascinated by the ways she danced and looked. She was beautiful and very well-dressed. I was sure she was English...

"She wore my clothes before we started working together. She wore one of my corset dresses to the premiere of *Desperately Seeking Susan*. When Madonna first called me in 1989, it was two days before my ready-to-wear show, and I thought my assistant was joking. I was a big fan. She asked me if I would do the ("Blond Ambition") tour. She knew what she wanted... a pinstripe suit, the feminine corsetry. Madonna likes my clothes because they combine the masculine and the feminine...

"She always knows what she wants. In the new ("Drowned World") show, there is a Spanish section and a kimono-geisha section. When I went to her wedding, which was in Scotland, I was in a kilt. And she said: 'I love your kilt. I want that in the show.'

"I felt a little bad (not to be asked to design the wedding dress). But I was very busy with planning my couture collection, so only a little. She looked very beautiful, like a little girl."

Domenico Dolce "She is fantastic, clever and full of ideas. She is very demanding about comfort... "

Stefano Gabbana "... and about cut and colour and proportion. She is our love, our inspiration."

Dolce & Gabbana "Madonna inspires our work in such a great manner. It's the ultimate satisfaction to dress her."

Madonna is a designer's dream. If she's wearing your clothes, you know you've made it. Here (opposite) Madonna hangs out with longtime collaborator Jean Paul Gaultier in New York in 1994. With her (above) are Dolce and Gabbana in Milan, October 1992, promoting *Sex* and *Erotica,* and (below) close friends Santo and Donatella, brother and sister of the late Gianni Versace.

Dean Caten "She doesn't miss a thing. She calculates how high she can lift her leg according to the weight of the pant and stuff like that. I remember one shirt we made a little bit bigger, and she noticed. She said, 'No, this is bigger, you changed it, make it the way it was.' We're talking about half a centimetre. She is very, very sharp."

Donatella Versace "Madonna changes images as rapidly as fashion and she's not afraid to take risks, and that makes her the single most important icon to fashion designers."

Maripol "Madonna is a child woman. She is vulnerable, then she is not. She'll survive anything."

Arianne Phillips, stylist: "It's a wholly collaborative process. Like everything with Madonna, it all comes initially from her ideas. Creating her costumes was just kind of a natural process. Over the past four years of working with Madonna, we've done so many different things. The 'Drowned World' tour was just an opportunity to relive some of those high points. She took what made sense and put it in the show...

"Everyone can pick a look from a famous designer, but Madonna can recontextualise a piece of clothing. Now that's glamorous."

Madonna on Gianni Versace (writing in *Time* magazine, November 1998): "The great yogis believe there is no end to life. I'm inclined to agree. Even though Gianni's life on this earth has ended, his spirit is everywhere and his soul lives forever. I'm going to miss you, Gianni. We're all going to miss you. But I've got a pocketful of memories in my Versace jeans, and they're not going anywhere."

Though the movie wasn't in the competition, Madonna hogged all the attention at the 1991 Cannes Film festival. Arriving for the midnight premiere of _In Bed With Madonna_ on May 13 at the Grand Theatre Lumiere, she paused at the top of the steps to show off her Gaultier bra and panties. Her party outfits (below) were not so becoming.

Madonna dyed her hair back to brown, and let it hang down straight. At a New York premiere party for _In Bed With Madonna_, she explained: "My chapters in my life don't begin with the colour of my hair. I suppose it is really a new chapter in my life because now I'm finally finished with the movie. This is kind of my farewell to it."

She said farewell at that particular party in a black satin gown worn over a sparkling, colourful basque, hold-up stockings and a shower of jewellery.

On the opposite coast, she held a celebratory party of her own, with proceeds going to an LA Aids charity in memory of Keith Haring and her early mentor, Christopher Flynn, who had both died from the disease.

At the Cannes film festival, with her hair (or a dark wig) worn up in sumptuous curls, she promoted the film with another striptease. A bolder and more surprising escapade than that at the Oscars, she simply dropped her pink, satin robe to the ground, smiling broadly as astonished industry big-wigs ogled her underwear – a satin Gaultier bra with cone cups and matching tight, flimsy shorts, panelled corset-like at the front.

But her bubble was about to burst. In February 1992, she received less than complimentary reviews for _Shadows And Fog_, the unmemorable Woody Allen picture in which a dark, curly-haired Madonna co-stars with Mia Farrow, John Malkovich and director Allen.

A League Of Their Own followed in the summer. A Forties baseball comedy also featuring Tom Hanks, Geena Davis and Rosie O'Donnell, it fared well at the box office but failed to endorse the respect Madonna had gained as a film star – although it did yield a hit single with 'This Used To Be My Playground'.

Now she was at work on the even more disastrous _Body Of Evidence_, while also completing a new album and a book. Together, these would cause unimagined problems... problems which all boiled down to sex. While Madonna continued to blaze a trail for personal freedom and to dramatize her bedroom fantasies, people were starting to ignore her. Some were getting bored. Others were unhappy at the preponderance of S&M imagery and the dubious implications of some of her visions.

"My chapters in my life don't begin with the colour of my hair"

Effortlessly, Madonna upstaged everybody at Cannes, including her former husband Sean Penn who was there to present _Indian Runner_ – his début as a director. She was photographed wherever she went, in her running gear and in her latest Gaultier creations. One particularly over-the-top ensemble teamed a serious jacket with a tutu, shorts, bootees and the pearl jewellery she had become so fond of lately.

As Executive Producer of _In Bed With Madonna_, she had invested $4 million of her own in the project. It was a box-office triumph, a critical success and an essential video in the collection of any self-respecting Madonna fan today. Apart from the satisfaction of making her money back, and more, she was thrilled at last to have become a one-hundred-per-cent genuine, solid-gold movie star.

The book, simply titled _Sex_, was published by Time-Warner in October 1992 in a large, slim format with stainless-steel covers. It was then distributed in silver wrapping to prevent potential buyers from simply flipping through it. Long since sold out, its pages are filled with explicit photographs and writings about sexual fantasy, attributable to Madonna and to an alter-ego, dominatrix character she names Dita.

The pictorial content features Madonna partially and fully undressed, taking part in a range of X-rated activities with models and celebrities including rapper Vanilla Ice (with whom she was said to have enjoyed some similar shenanigans in real life), supermodel Naomi Campbell, actress and friend Isabella Rosselini, rapper Big Daddy Kane and the ubiquitous Tony Ward.

Madonna waxes lyrical all the way through her personal *Kama Sutra*, composing joyful odes to her vagina, singing the praises of anal sex and working herself into a lather over domination and submission. Dipping into *Sex*'s visual treasure trove, the reader meets with foot fetishism, shaving, lesbianism, homosexuality, straight sex, oral sex and, controversially, a rape scenario in which Madonna, dressed as a schoolgirl, is held down and abused by skinheads.

This was a step too far for many of her fans, particularly the feminists who had previously given Madonna the benefit of the doubt. She had convinced them that her erotic costumes were the choices of an assertive woman rather than the

trappings of a male plaything, that women could be both strong and sexy, and that her role-play upheld a woman's right to declare her sexuality in whatever form it should take, a right to *take control*. Madonna, they had always felt, was leading by example, helping to empower women sexually as she had clearly empowered herself.

Rape scenes were something else. Madonna retorted that the photograph depicted a sexual enactment that had earlier been agreed by the three willing parties. Indeed, she claimed, she had been raped herself during her first year in New York, and therefore understood the devastating reality.

Photographer Steven Meisel was one of Madonna's

Though she shines in her videos, real movie stardom has evaded Madonna thus far. A small role in Woody Allen's *Shadows And Fog* as a circus acrobat (main picture) was largely overlooked, though her starring role in *Basic Instinct*-wannabe *Body Of Evidence* as art gallery owner Rebecca Carlson (top) was trashed. She enjoyed more success with a minor role as man-hungry baseball player Mae Mordabito in 1992's *A League Of Their Own* (centre), though Uli Edel's *Dangerous Games* (bottom) was poorly received.

Gay Times

Girls wanted to *be* Madonna. Guys wanted to make love to Madonna. And for someone who appealed so vividly to a heterosexual audience, it may have seemed unusual that she should equally enthrall the men and women of the gay community.

But this was Madonna. It really wasn't surprising at all.

She'd been bending genders, blending genders, mixing up the rules and the roles so comprehensively that her sexuality held out something fascinating for everyone.

At all times, she insisted: if it feels good, do it, but do it safely.

Mistress of imagination and fantasy, she was tough and timid, aggressive and passive, strong and sensitive, masculine and feminine, macho and camp, a beautiful goddess, a sex kitten in underwear, a dominatrix, a dyke, a drag queen, a cover girl.

If it feels good, do it, do it safely, do it your way, and do it another way too if you fancy it. Express yourself! Free your fantasies! Do not fear!

Madonna once stated: "Just about everything in the world is centred around sexual attraction and sexual power."

Understanding that and, some might say, understanding how it could successfully be applied to her career, Madonna became sexually attractive and powerful to as many people as possible – which is not to imply that her sentiments were not heartfelt or to try to invalidate her dramatisations.

She had long been sending out bisexual signals, from her stories of childhood frolics with girlfriends such as Moira McFarland through her ambiguous relationships with Sandra Bernhard and Ingrid Casares, her famous lesbian kisses and her erotic poses with women in the *Sex* book.

She told Norman Mailer: "There are times I really feel bisexual... I just think it's important to fuck what you want to fuck and not feel shame about it."

But as time went on, she began to remove the mystery. "I'm not a lesbian, but I thought it was undignified to say so," she declared. "So what if I was? I'm not going to say that I've never slept with a woman, but I love men."

Some feminists were suspicious of Madonna, her professed bisexuality and her male-baiting underwear as outerwear.

Madonna countered that strength of character comes from self-expression and freedom of choice. She added: "To call me an anti-feminist is ludicrous... I think in the Fifties, women weren't ashamed of their bodies. They luxuriated in their sexuality and being strong in their femininity. I think that is better than hiding it and saying, 'I'm strong, I'm just like a man.' Women aren't like men. They can do things men can't do...

"I don't think about the work I do in terms of feminism. I certainly feel that I give women strength and hope, particularly young women. So in that respect, I feel my behaviour is feminist or my art is feminist. But I'm certainly not militant about it, nor do I exactly pre-meditate it."

Many feminist women were, of course, on Madonna's side, endorsing her status as a role model par excellence, and, sometimes, as a fantasy lover.

In 1993, Thames And Hudson published an extraordinary book called *I Dream Of Madonna: Women's Dreams Of The Goddess Of Pop*. Dedicated "to Madonna and to the Madonna in you", it contained descriptions of fifty intimate and often erotic dreams about the star by ordinary, young and middle-aged women.

Even after motherhood and a second marriage, she is still creating headlines such as the *Daily Star*'s "Madonna 'Picked Up Girl Stripper'" on July 19, 2001 – a tale denied by her representative who added, with a touch of the old flash: "I don't know if it's anything she'd be ashamed of."

Undoubtedly, Madonna would be proud to know that, following her example, contemporary female performers including Geri Halliwell and Kylie Minogue are happy to stage lesbian-themed presentations.

Traditionally, however, Madonna has had more in common with gay men, whose company she has sought, enjoyed and learned from since her earliest experiences of nightlife in Michigan. "Obviously, in the dance world, I was surrounded by gay men and going to gay nightclubs. That's where I started to feel good about myself and didn't feel like I had to look a certain way."

The self-confessed "fag-hag poster child" told the *Guardian*: "I'm sure that's really influenced me, because from the dance world to the music world, my social strata was really gay men. That's who my audience was, that's who I hung out with, that's who inspired me. For me, it freed me, because I could do and be whatever I wanted. So the problem arose when I left that world and went into the mainstream. Suddenly there was judgement."

Amusing her supporters with proclamations like, "Every straight guy should have a man's tongue in his mouth at least once," Madonna went on to a perfectly suitable part in *The Next Best Thing*. Not only did she become pregnant with her gay best friend (Rupert Everett), but she insisted that her character should be a yoga teacher and not the swimming instructor originally written into the script.

However, Madonna's importance to the gay male is more nostalgic, less vital these days as she mellows into heterosexual domesticity.

Madonna has frequently espoused gay rights, granting outspoken interviews to magazines like *The Advocate* – in which she insisted that "every straight guy should have a man's tongue in his mouth at least once" – and hiring an almost exclusively homosexual cast of dancers for her 1990 Blond Ambition tour. She has worked tirelessly for AIDS charities, and regularly appears at the LA Danceathon events (below).

Why Gay Men Loved Her

One who loved was Peter Robinson, a twenty-four-year-old pop writer in London. These are his reasons.

1 "She's a fantastic bitch, so single-minded in her pursuit of being famous."

2 "She's been very good to us. Some of her first gigs were in gay clubs, establishing that she was very much part of that scene."

3 "I don't think she's done it deliberately, but she has very good reference points. She worked with people like Nick Kamen (the jeans model turned singer) who had a big gay following, and the kind of music she was making – disco – was a very gay music."

"She wasn't overly feminine. There were points where she wasn't shaving her armpits, and she became quite muscular. Obviously, she's really beautiful. She's the kind of girl gay men find attractive if they do find women attractive at all. **4** She has a very masculine jawline and she's never really attempted to disguise that – 'This is what I'm like, I'm not going to change for you and I'm gonna be in your face.' She's uncompromising about her identity."

5 "She has supported Aids victims and charities. She must have known a lot of people who died, people who were close to her heart, and she knows a lot of the fans who put her where she is today are likely to be affected by that – 'I'm going to do what I can for them.'"

"People liked the intrigue of not knowing what her sexuality really was. She kept a lot of herself back. She didn't feel that she had to give all of herself to everyone all the time. But now **6** she's quite straight. She's a family woman with kids, so that over-rides the old fascination – 'Oh, maybe she's a bit of a part-time lesbian.'"

7 "Her music was great, but she's gone in a different direction. If her last two albums had been her first two albums, I don't think she'd have the same gay following."

"*What I wrote*

about S&M

was supposed

to be amusing"

Madonna's new image, unveiled in October 1992, was a surprise to even the most hardened observer. Dressed in fetish uniform and brandishing a rider's crop, Madonna also showcased a gold front tooth, engraved with the initial D. This stood for Madonna's new alter ego, a French good-time girl called Dita Parlo...

favourites. He had set her up in a series of classic Monroe poses for *Vanity Fair* early in 1991, wearing sleek Norma Kawali dresses, Marilyn's original blouse and black, satin skirt from the 1956 film *Bus Stop* and, in the famous photo spread with the Ralph Lauren sheet, nothing at all. In the same year, the pair had joined forces on a *Rolling Stone* collection called "Flesh And Fantasy", picturing Madonna in scenes of lesbianism, drag and group sex, dressed in stockings, suspenders and stilettoes.

There was no denying the excellence of the photography in *Sex*, but many reviewers found the subject matter vulgar, seedy, cheap, obvious and rife with humiliation and degradation.

Madonna defended her work by declaring that she intended the images to be viewed as products of the imagination, existing in a wonderful fantasy world rather than in the mean streets of real life where people were dying of Aids. Her aim, she said, was to encourage personal exploration, not promiscuity.

She also claimed that much of the text had been misconstrued: "What I wrote about S&M was supposed to be amusing. It was never meant to be this incredibly hot, arousing, erotic piece of porn. In fact, I was poking fun at everybody's prejudices about other people's sexuality and their own sexuality."

As the furore raged on, Madonna, simultaneously, released an aural accompaniment – her new album, *Erotica*, which carried photographs from *Sex* and also dwelled at length on the pleasures of the flesh. Co-written and co-produced with dance master and 'Vogue' collaborator Shep Pettibone with the intention of stepping into contemporary grooves, the album – for all its merit – was seriously overshadowed by the rumpus over *Sex*, clocking up only a couple of million sales, although it did burn very brightly for five minutes.

This was because of the video for the mesmerising hit 'Erotica', the first single. Illustrating the theme of pain as pleasure, the clip introduces Madonna in character as macho dominatrix Dita, wearing an S&M mask and a gold tooth. Complete with another lesbian kiss, the film was outlawed before midnight by MTV.

It would be her last video venture into hard sex: Madonna changed her tactics in response to the backlash that had erupted over the *Sex* book, the *Erotica* album and her latest movie, *Body Of Evidence*, which reached the silver screen early in 1993.

The plot centres on the death of an older lover after a sex bout with Madonna, and her subsequent affair with her lawyer. Her performance was savaged by critics, who drew their knives again when she followed on with the sexfest that was Dangerous Game.

It was time to cool it, and the videos that Madonna released throughout 1993 benefited from the urgency for fresh ideas, which arrived either as narratives or innovative visual effects.

'Bad Girl', the tale of a smoking, drinking, female executive who can't help sleeping with strangers, assumes the proportions of a modern-day ghost story as guardian spirit Christopher Walken snatches our heroine from her deathbed and carries her off on a cloud to an eternity of happiness and cigarillos.

There's little flamboyance here about Madonna, who switches from a black office outfit with a white, wide-collared blouse to a dark winter coat and hat and some fairly conservative evening wear, again in black. Back to blonde, her hair flounces free around her shoulders, although there's an unusual timidity about her make-up. Thinly plucked eyebrows arch over shades of gleaming pink, little if anything in the way of liner, and rose-pink lips.

She's even more sparsely made-up in the 'Fever' promo, with pale, pearly eye highlighter, the faint shading of a socket line and light-pink lipstick giving her face the appearance of a blank canvas, surrounded by extremely short and startling red hair. Nothing else about Madonna is blank, though. She dances in a variety of outfits, including two red tops, a pair of tight, velvety trousers and a figure-hugging gold mini-dress, appearing elsewhere as an Eastern goddess with long, spiked fingernails and a near-naked flower child, fringes hanging from her arms and blossoms covering her three points of modesty.

The most dramatic feature of 'Fever' is Madonna's first all-out use of computer technology, enabling her to be transformed into an extraordinary creature made of shimmering, molten metal, a favourite technique of director and fashion photographer Stephen Sednaoui, who had previously painted the Red Hot Chilli Peppers in a similar style.

Much more tranquil is the award-winning, futuristic, and very *blue* video accompanying 'Rain', which was originally filmed in black and white and then hand-painted to create the vivid colourings. Here, Madonna achieves an almost icy beauty with blue-black hair, bright blue eyes and a long, dark shift-dress, changing to white against a blue-black skyscape.

Along the way, she kisses her male co-star, briefly getting nude with him, while a make-up artist attends to her face. A touch of blusher and a pair of false but unobtrusive lashes form the basis of Madonna's latest concession to subtlety.

The force of her determination to rethink her style, not this time as a whim but as a necessity, would affect almost every aspect of her performance, and the winds of change were blowing forcefully through the ballpark when Madonna set forth in the autumn of 1993 with "The Girlie Show".

Let's Face It

Make-up artist **Laura Mercier** had this to say of Madonna: "When she looks at herself with Eighties big hair and make-up and eyebrows like a forest, of course she laughs at herself. But she doesn't regret it; it was part of what she had to go through. Why should she be ashamed? It's part of a woman's evolution."

Madonna's evolution as far as cosmetics go has been a particularly colourful one. Not only has her make-up formed an integral part of each image she has presented to the public, it has also been a crucial ingredient in her stagecraft.

From her earliest ragamuffin days with black rings of kohl and thick, heavily pencilled eyebrows to the pale foundation, thinly plucked eyebrows, lightly shadowed eyes and red lipstick of *Evita*, from the bronzed shading and gold highlighting of the *Music* cowgirl to the sleek sophistication of today's subtle shades and techniques, she has used her make-up to create a co-ordinated impact with her hair, clothes, accessories and jewellery.

She may well look back and laugh: the "big hair and make-up and eyebrows like a forest" were exuberant DIY, like the rubber bangles and the tights and scarves she wrapped round her head, and they looked top heavy, detracting from the lower part of her face. The Forties style restored the balance, the red lipstick redirecting the focus to her lips, and providing a fuller appearance. The bronze and gold look was more flattering still, picking out the cheek and brow bones, while Madonna's current, straight, blonde hairstyle sets off her preferred skin tones – chic, glowing beige and pink, with just enough shadow, liner, highlighter and mascara to create dramatic eyes.

Some of her onstage recreations – the geisha or Monroe, for instance – have presented her make-up artist with a more particular challenge.

Laura Mercier, who specializes in "the flawless face", has worked with top cosmetics companies, designers, photographers, magazines, models and actresses. She told the *Telegraph*:

"Madonna is such a perfectionist and it is very exciting translating her ideas into an all-over look. Unlike some of the people I work with, she is never late and always makes time for her make-up to be done properly.

"Over the years, we have done many different looks, including ironic, dark and smoky S&M images, and also a pretty, feminine feel... During the day she keeps it very light. She concentrates on the skin, the brows are defined and the lips are brown rose or stained raspberry."

Madonna endorsed one of the lipsticks in Laura's own make-up range, a dark burgundy shade called "M".

But she gave more than her name and her approval to Max Factor in 1999 when she appeared in a television advertisement, broadcast in Europe and Asia, for the company's Gold line of lipsticks and foundation.

Max Factor himself was the first person ever to create make-up for the movies, replacing the old, sweaty greasepaint with something more pleasing. He transformed the likes of Garbo and Gloria Swanson for the silver screen, and was soon the darling of A-list actresses including Joan Crawford, Bette Davis, Lana Turner, Rita Hayworth and Elizabeth Taylor.

A Max Factor spokeswoman said of the Madonna campaign: "We wanted to take the brand forward while going back to what we are all about – supreme glamour. There was only one woman able to carry that message into the 21st Century...

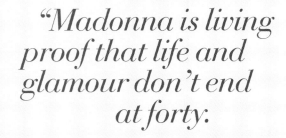

"Madonna is living proof that life and glamour don't end at forty.

The endorsement is a stronger statement coming from someone with maturity, gravitas and the life experience to back it up."

Using that life experience, Madonna insisted on approving the script, the cast, the crew and every detail of her own appearance, from her hair to her Versace clothes. The ad was very simple: Madonna sat on a movie set having her make-up done, joking with real-life cosmetic artist Sarah Monzani and her usual hairdresser, Luigi Murencu. After applying the Max Factor lipstick, her screen embrace with a gorgeous actor carried on after the call of "Cut!"

The intention was to reveal both the "real" Madonna and the superstar.

These days, Madonna is apparently still using Laura Mercier mascara and foundation, Nars beige shadow and pink blusher, and hip products by Toni and Tina. She is a fan of Dr Hauschka's organic skincare range for cleansing, toning, moisturising and creaming, based on aromatherapy, and is said to enjoy Dr Hauschka facials in Knightsbridge with best friends Gwyneth Paltrow and Stella McCartney, at £89 per two-hour treatment.

For special pampering, she likes the rooftop health club and spa at London's Berkeley Hotel, with its Dior beauty treatments. This costs £50 for the facilities, plus another £50 for a half-hour massage. Madonna also visits the facilities at the Sanderson Hotel, which offers facials, reflexology, shiatsu, massage and hydrotherapy among other more exotic-sounding treatments. Legend has it that she further treats her skin by coating it with honey before taking a bath.

It's also believed that Madonna has her own scents created by Oliver Creed, at the cost of £12,500 a visit, and she's said to have had a scent custom-made for her by Francoise Rapp of Arom'Alchemy, who combines the benefits of aromatherapy with traditional perfumery.

In Bed With Madonna **director Alek Keshishian was responsible for photography and direction on the ultra-glamorous 1999 Max Factor campaign, which yielded images similar in style to the paintings of her favourite artist, Tamara De Lempicka.**

Her favourite manicurist, when she's in America, is Louis Mattassi, and she patronises various London salons. She favours OPI nail lacquer, reportedly wearing their Italian Love Affair shade at her wedding to Guy Ritchie.

It's also been stated that she'd die without red Chanel varnish for her toenails.

Meanwhile, London hair colourist Daniel Galvin has set off a celebrity trend called Pop Colour, following his work with Madonna. On her last visit to his West End salon, she had her hair rinsed with his Miracle Solution Highlight Brightener before the colours were added – pale gold to the strands around her face and deepening shades further back. She has had her locks tended by celebrity cutter Sam McKnight.

There has been no confirmation of tabloid speculation in February 2001 that Madonna has had cosmetic surgery in London to remove bags from under her eyes.

3: THE RESURRECTION **1993–2001**

It had a whole different feel. That much was evident from the first moments, when fairground music burst happily out of the speakers and dizzy, coloured lights danced round the stage.

The emphasis of "The Girlie Show", opening in London in September 1993, was on fun. Well, adult fun. Madonna had not turned into Mother Superior overnight – she had plenty of provocative, new underwear to show off, her dance routines were as sizzling as ever, and she still had a point or two to make. But it was all more of a saucy circus, a knockabout revue, than a seriously sexual undertaking.

Dispensing with the conical cups, the harsh S&M overtones and the heaving, solo orgasms of "Blond Ambition", Madonna introduced a more light-hearted eroticism. The costumes – many created with Dolce & Gabbana – were spectacular rather than outrageous, and even dressed as Dita, she was playful, mischievous, clearly little threat to the nation's youth.

But for all the frivolity of the new show, Madonna had come to town with her hardest look to date. Her hair was blonde and cropped closely to her head and round the ears, with a side parting; her face was sternly made up with thin, sweeping stokes of eyebrow pencil, darkly defined socket lines, purple eye gloss, lots of black around the lashes, and dark plum lipstick.

Roll up! Roll up! It was, she trumpeted, "the greatest show on earth!"

This was entertainment in the grand old tradition, right down to the joshing around at the end where she feigned indignation that the set was over and staged mock-struggles with the spoilsport dancers trying to lead her offstage.

There were girls as well as boys in the dance troupe, performing acrobatics up and down a rope ladder during 'The Beast Within'. There were elements of mime, a jack-in-the-box clown character and a touch of time-honoured bantering with the audience – "I can't hear you!" Religious comment was kept to a minimum in a production which highlighted the infectious joviality of 'I'm Going Bananas' and the Dietrich impersonations of 'Like A Virgin'.

In a hilariously over-the-top revision, 'Like A Virgin' was delivered with heavy, Germanic enunciation and incorporated a few lines from 'Falling In Love Again'. She was dressed as the legendary actress too, with a black suit, a white shirt, a scarf tightly wrapped round her head, a shiny, black top hat and a cane.

She stayed with the outfit for 'Bye Bye Baby', in which she kissed one of her similarly clad female dancers, grabbed her own crotch and cracked, "We fuck women? We do?" Furthering the gender play, she had some of her male dancers squeezed into colourful basques. Then, sticking with the pants, she ditched the jacket to reveal a stripy, short-sleeved top for a romp through 'I'm Going Bananas'.

It wasn't the first time she had borrowed from the famously butch Dietrich, who was at the same time extremely beautiful – a combination guaranteed to intrigue Madonna.

In a separate part of "The Girlie Show", she again paid tribute to the star, incorporating masculine and feminine in an outfit featuring a white shirt with huge, lacy cuffs, a waistcoat, a black, polka-dotted necktie and a dark, tiered skirt with a bustle. An eye patch, a pair of opera glasses and the inevitable top hat completed the look with which she performed 'Justify My Love'.

The concert opened with a tease, the audience believing that the spotlit, topless lady writhing down a pole in a G-string to the stage was Madonna. She herself came on as Dita, sliding a rider's crop between her legs and cavorting on the floor as she performed 'Erotica' in *Cabaret* mode with sequins shimmering across her black fringed top, bra and belted shorts. She added fishnet tights, a pair of inordinately clumpy, knee-length, shiny, lace-up boots with stacked heels, and three-quarter-length gloves – a favourite accessory.

Two male dancers paraded enormous muscles in black trunks and boots like Madonna's for 'Fever', bumping and grinding against each other and her as she tantalisingly wiggled her breasts and hips. The cover song – her most successful single of recent times – came to an end in a burst of flames.

The greatest *show* on earth

She donned an elaborate head-dress for 'Vogue' and changed into a bra with strings of beads for straps – an effective use of jewellery and one which she had showcased in 1989's *Bloodhounds Of Broadway*, wearing an all-pearl, tasselled bra-and-pants ensemble, with matching head decoration. (Dark-haired and festooned with exotic jewellery, she was perfect for the part of a Damon Runyan Twenties showgirl but it was a disappointing film which received only a limited run before being hastily transferred to video.)

For 'Rain', Madonna wore a long, dark gown with a plunging cleavage before disappearing to ready herself for the rumbustious central section of the show – a *Hair*-inspired extravaganza of songs, dance and free love for all, both gays and straights.

As 'Express Yourself' began, she descended to the stage on a glitter ball, joining her dancers in a frizzy, white Afro wig, a multi-coloured mini-top with fringes and generous displays of midriff and leg. Not her most flattering outfit, it endowed her with all the seductiveness of a Vera Duckworth at Woodstock, but she stripped to her bra all the same for 'Deeper And Deeper' – a riot of brightly coloured boas and bellbottoms.

Mournful in her bra and sequinned shorts for 'In This Life' and smart in military greatcoat with its epaulettes and big, brassy buttons for 'Holiday', she brought the show to an end with 'Everybody Is A Star'/'Everybody' wearing pale shorts and a simple green and yellow V-neck shirt, which she hitched up into a bra-revealing top.

The Girlie Show opened in London on September 25, 1993. Perhaps in response to the bashing she had received for her overtly sexual exploits of the last few years, the show was a family-friendly cabaret, with only the odd dash of controversy. She showed off a harsh new haircut (opposite), which contrasted superbly with the blonde afro wig she wore for 'Express Yourself' and 'Deeper And Deeper' (below).

Madonna reinterpreted 'Vogue' as a Balinese burlesque for the Girlie Show, making full use of the catwalk that extended into the front rows of the audience. During the routine, she walked over the backs of her prostrate male dancers, confirming her position as dominatrix diva.

GIRLIE

A Stylist's View

Polly Gordon, a London stylist organizing clothes for modelling shoots and music videos, looks at Madonna's career in fashion.

What do you admire most about Madonna?

"I think she's really clever, 'cos she's worked with really good people – Gaultier, Dolce & Gabbana, Gucci – at exactly the time they were right for her. She's always on the case. And the designers all say she's got a very big hand in everything they do, so she's nobody's fool.

"I like the idea that even in her earliest days, she was working with people like Keith Haring, a real cult artist. She was already making her connections, and she always looked so confident.

"She's probably incredibly aware of lighting and camera work, and I'm sure she has the final say in most things. I know that in one video, they had amazing beauty lighting, and she asked for her appearance not to look so perfect cos she wasn't twenty any more."

What has made Madonna such a fashion phenomenon?

"She's ahead of the game. She's really good at picking up on things, like the customised T-shirts recently. She sees what's around and then she can go out and look like she's setting a trend, and she does.

"Also, she's been very clever about what people could manage to copy. It's aspirational. When she had all her bangles and rubber bracelets and crop-tops, you could have a Madonna look without having to be dressed head to toe in designer clothes.

"She has the best people around her to make her look fabulous. She doesn't do anything half-heartedly. She's full-on, but she can take it. She doesn't look scared, even in her most outrageous outfits. She's completely in control of her image."

What have been her problems over the years?

"I think people have missed the point sometimes. They've taken her too seriously and overlooked her sense of humour. She's so famous that whatever she does, there'll be people knocking her.

"Also, she's a really little person (five feet four) and to make a big impact, her stage outfits have to be over the top. If you look at the polka-dot bolero outfit with all the ruffles that she wore in 'Blond Ambition', it's not that great, her hair is really severe and she's wearing very hard make-up, I don't think it's her most attractive look, but it's a stage outfit and it's quite stunning. You do remember it."

What were her brightest ideas?

"The bras were a really smart move. When she dies, you'll pick up a picture of Madonna and she'll be in a big bra. The idea of underwear as outerwear is still very current. You see sheer tops that incorporate the bra. Dolce & Gabbana are doing a flowery, chiffon dress that the bra is attached to. And no one's afraid of having a lot of buttons undone any more.

"Chloe was a smart move too. She's actually taken on the look of the Chloe girl. Stella McCartney did a lot for Chloe. She's so on the case for the trendy girl-around-town."

What could Madonna possibly do next?

"She's done so much. The thing you noticed about the "Drowned World" tour was how much stuff she's taken from around the world – the Spanish look, the Japanese thing with the really major kimono and the make-up, and the kung-fu section. She did the Seventies London punk and the cowgirl thing – 'Hey, y'all!' Before that, she had all the Indian influence, the Eastern philosophies and the religion, so she *became* it. One minute she's got this short blonde hair, the next she's got long, straggly hair, henna on the hands and her leg behind her head. She looks at different cultures, takes something and runs with it. She's going to run out of continents!"

Is Madonna still capable of setting another trend?

"Yes, cos she works with young people. I can't think of any other older stars who have the guts to do it. Janet Jackson hasn't really moved on. But I'm sure Madonna is a voracious reader of underground magazines, and she'll find designers that are up and coming. They're on the cutting edge of what's going on, so therefore *she* is. She takes inspiration from everyone around her. I think she'd be a fantastic person to work with."

The Best ... the Worst

PAPA DON'T PREACH
"I love her hair short. This was really brave, cos it was such a move away from all that hair and the earrings and stuff. It was her first major change of style. The "Italians do it better" T-shirt is a complete classic."

THE LITTLE BLACK DRESS
"I think she looks a bit cheap, and it seems like she's got too much make-up on. She was wearing horrific shoes as well, really clumpy, horrible ones."

THE GAULTIER SUIT
"This is quite hardcore. It's really masculine, but at the same time, it's showing off your bosoms and being quite strong about it. I like the contrast. It's really mixing genders."

MARLENE DIETRICH
"It's quite a hard, East German look. She often added bowler hats and monocles. She can do some really butch things. It helped her in a way, like it didn't do David Bowie any harm to have people whispering that he was gay. But Madonna is such a man's woman, this butchness is just another costume for her."

MARIE ANTOINETTE
"At Madonna's level of achievement, you don't have to prove your image, so you can have a laugh with it. It's a bit of an Elton John thing – 'I've done this song "Vogue" thirty times in the black outfit and I fancy doing something different.'"

DAME EDNA EVERIDGE
"It's the outfit wearing *her*, which is really unusual. She has everything but the kitchen sink on there, and she's so lost behind it. It looks really awkward."

EVITA
"It's really beautiful. She flirted with the Forties look around the time of the film. I like the way she does it completely with the hat, the make-up, everything. Her lips are soft, not the harsh red she wore so much before. It's the beginning of showing that she can 'do grown-up' as well as being in touch with younger people. Maybe she wanted to be taken seriously as an actress."

ON GAULTIER'S CATWALK
"I don't think it's really attractive. She's done Gaultier a favour here. I've never seen her wearing anything like that anywhere else. It's a really Thirties look with the thin, high brows. She doesn't look nervous about having her breasts out, but it's better when she's completely in control. In the *Sex* book, she looks really beautiful with them out, because she's creating the image."

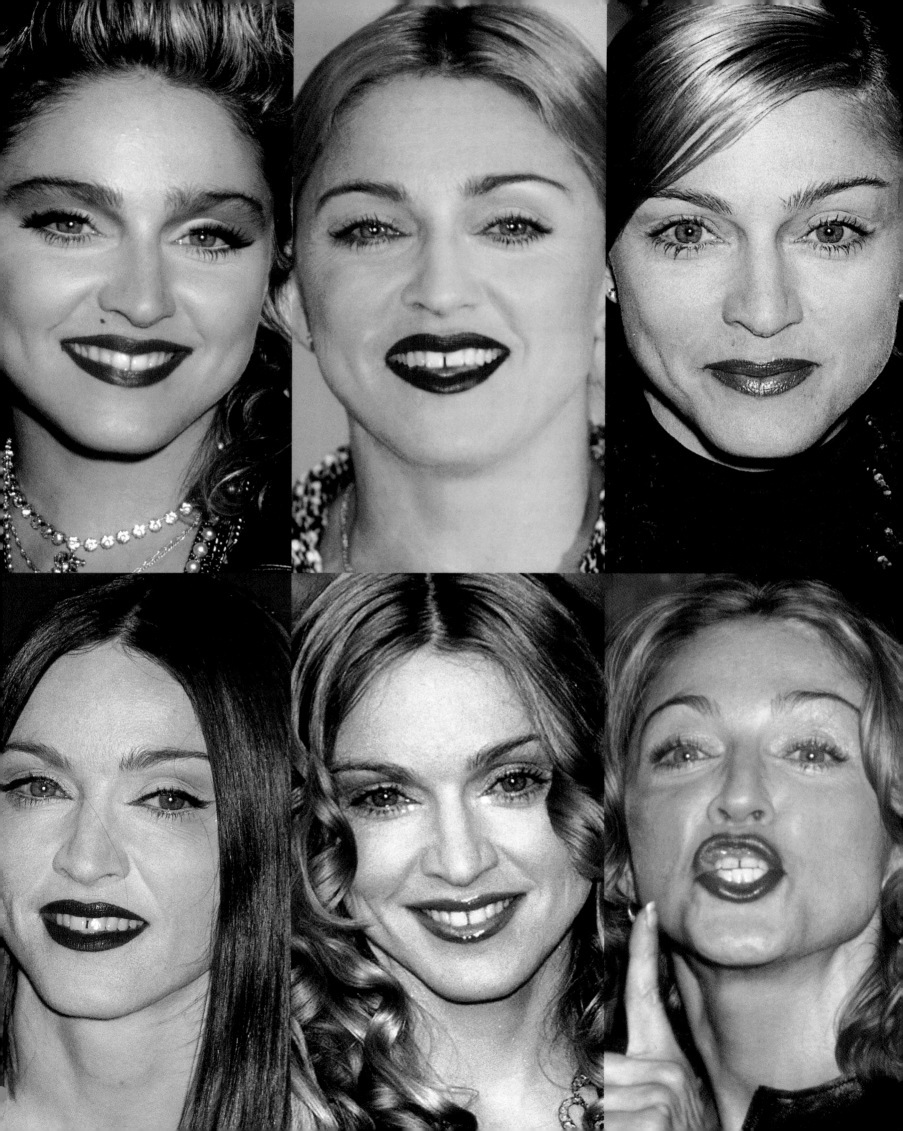

"The Girlie Show" was hugely enjoyed by fans and press alike around the world. However, Madonna lost a lot of admirers in March 1994 with what they considered to be an unacceptably coarse appearance on *The Late Show With David Letterman* – although she won some new converts with her foul-mouthed exchanges, notoriously using the F-word thirteen times.

By way of introduction, Letterman introduced Madonna as "one of the biggest stars in the world," who had "slept with some of the biggest names in the entertainment industry". Walking on, dark-haired in a tight, black dress and combat boots, she gave as good as she got.

"Aren't you going to smell them?" she demanded of Letterman after handing him a pair of knickers and describing him as "twisted" and "a sick fuck". And that was just for openers. Smoking a cigar and referring to the panties more than once as the banter between herself and Letterman grew more bizarre, Madonna finally demanded: "Did you know that it's good if you pee in the shower?"

Scarcely believing what he'd heard, Letterman blurted out, "I'm sorry?"

"No, seriously... " rattled on Madonna. "Peeing in the shower is really good. It... it fights, um, um, athlete's foot. I'm serious, no, urine is like, is like... is like an antiseptic. It's all got to do with the enzymes in your body."

a yuppie version of Beavis and Butt-Head, you know – 'Oooooh, gross.'

"I don't think he knew what he was getting into, but once he realized how the show went, the next day, instead of just saying, 'We had a good time, it was all good fun and completely consensual,' maybe the networks freaked out and he didn't want to fall from grace from them, so he went with the gestalt of the media and said, 'Yeah, it was really disgusting and, yes, she really behaved badly,' and turned it into something else to save face."

Years on, Madonna admitted that maybe it hadn't been all good, rude fun after all. She told *TV Guide* magazine, "That was a time in my life when I was extremely angry. Angry with the way I was brought up. Angry about how sexist this society that we live in is. Angry with people who assumed that because I had a sexuality that I couldn't also be talented. Just everything. The press was completely beating up on me and I felt like a victim. So I lashed out at people, and that night was one of those times. And I am not particularly proud of it."

This confession bore similarities to Madonna's later explanation of her reasons for *Sex*. Despite the general assumption that she had made her peace with Tony Ciccone, she once again acknowledged the ghosts of her past when she said of her book: "It was my own personal rebellion against my father, against the way I was raised, against the culture, against society, against everything. It was just a huge, massive act of rebellion."

"I just had the best time, and I actually thought he was having a good time, too"

"Don't you know a good pharmacist?" flashed back Letterman, who then tried to wind up the interview. But the lady wasn't for moving.

"Oh, oh, oh, and pee in the shower," she persisted. "Don't tell me you haven't peed in the shower. Everybody pees in the shower and everybody picks their nose."

By now, members of the studio audience were heckling, calling for Madonna to "Get off!"

She later claimed that the producers had encouraged her to act and talk as she did, but had changed their tune when the flak began to fly. Months later, she told Norman Mailer: "Since the David Letterman show, the news is that I've lost my mind."

She added: "Before I went on the show, all his writers were coming in my dressing room, giving me tons of stuff they wanted me to say and it was all so insulting... So in my mind, he knew that that's what the game plan was, that we were going to fuck with each other on TV. I told some of the writers I was going to swear, and they went, 'Oh, great, do it, we'll bleep it and it'll be hysterical.' I just had the best time, and I actually thought he was having a good time, too. But he's kind of like

Clearly, while Madonna was taking strides away from theoutrage which had helped to launch her career, her firecracker spirit was still liable to burst into controversy.

There were raised eyebrows, again, when she posed on the cover of Esquire at the end of that summer in a rubber bikini with a dog chain and lead round her neck. She also revealed her latest jewellery – nose and belly button piercings. Explaining these to Norman Mailer, who wrote the piece, she described the nostril ring as "just another adornment".

Mailer commented: "On my stuffy side, I thought: If I had a ring in my nose, it would take me two minutes to get it all cleaned out."

"It doesn't take me two minutes," retorted Madonna. "I just have to blow my nose carefully. It's nice to have to think about something that you take for granted."

The author further wanted to know if it could cause injury to her during kissing.

"That's the beauty of it," she responded. "You have to be careful. It's like, well, someone could hurt my nose. It's like riding a motorcycle without a helmet. It's just a risk. In the most simplistic way, it's just another way to take a chance."

Madonna outraged viewers (above) with her appearance on the David Letterman show in 1994, letting loose a string of expletives and prompting David to sniff her panties. In London's Hyde Park Hotel (opposite) in October 1992, promoting 'Erotica' and Sex, Madonna dealt with provocative issues in a much more restrained manner, speaking often of her "art". The look is pure Dietrich, down to the distinctly unfeminine cigar.

The Fans

EMMA JOHNSTON, a 23-year-old rock writer from London, has been a Madonna fan for more than a decade.

Favourite songs 'Like A Virgin', 'Like A Prayer', 'Material Girl' and 'Ray Of Light', but it depends on the day and what mood I'm in.

Favourite video 'Like A Prayer', definitely.

Favourite era I do like Eighties Madonna, just because she seemed to be determined to prove herself all the time, just constantly pushing herself to get to the top and stay there. Which she managed.

Favourite outfits There are so many! I can maybe narrow it down to the 'Express Yourself' suit and the 'Material Girl' pink dress.

Favourite Madonna moment Most of them. I think the whole of *In Bed With Madonna* was good. And seeing her at Brixton.

What's special about Madonna Just the way she makes the most of her talents and has manipulated them to create this superstar. She maybe doesn't have the best voice in the world, but she has the star quality that most other singers don't have. It's mainly just the fact that she seems to have so much drive, and the way she's done everything for herself, dragging herself up from the boots. I'm sure she used people and manipulated them on the way, but her determination and hard work, and the way she totally runs the whole show in what was when she started (and still is, to a certain extent) a male-dominated environment. She used her sexuality to get what she wanted, but she never seemed like a victim or an object for people to lust after – she's always the one in charge. And she's capable of changing without it looking forced or desperate. She's gone from being a PVC-clad dominatrix to a respectable mum with no one thinking the changes are anything but absolutely right for her.

Inspiration She's an inspiration to anyone with ambition... Just the way she's gone out and done it all for herself, from the performances to the business deals to the hiring and firing, and has managed to keep up with herself.

PENNY McKINLEY, a 29-year-old-marketing manager from London, has been a Madonna fan for 17 years.

Favourite songs 'Rain', 'I'll Remember' and 'Into The Groove' would all be main contenders.

Favourite video 'Take A Bow', 'Like A Prayer' and 'Material Girl'.

Favourite era Without a doubt the *Like A Prayer/In Bed With Madonna* era.

Favourite outfits I loved what she wore to the Cannes Film Festival when she was promoting *In Bed With Madonna*, the pink robe and the cone bra. She looked elegant as well as retaining that individual "Madonna Style". And she was a brunette at the time as well, which I think really suits her.

Favourite Madonna moment Every moment of *In Bed With Madonna*. This has got to be one of my favourite videos.

What's special about Madonna She is the original Girl Power as far as I'm concerned. She was openly immodest about her ambition. She didn't care about criticisms of the way she looked – in fact, she set out to shock and push the boundaries. She represented everything I wanted to be but knew I was not. I had the crucifix and the lacy stuff, but I never wore cropped tops or showed off my bra. I was a conservative wannabe!

Inspiration She makes me feel anything is possible so long as you are willing to put in the hard work and dedication. Oh, and it helps if you don't give a damn!

ANGIE HUNG, a 24-year-old internet project manager and would-be actress from Calgary, Canada, has always been a casual admirer of Madonna, but became a major fan in 1995.

Favourite songs 'Like A Prayer' because it combines a sensual and spiritual urgency. It's so rare that a song can leave the listener feeling blessed, weary, joyful and scared all at the same time. I don't confess to understanding the lyrics, but it's the production and aura as a whole that leave me in awe.

Favourite video 'Open Your Heart'. I have always been fascinated by the dichotomy between youth and being an "adult".

Favourite era The one right now. The Madonna that makes her family and children the top priority. The one that sings about a 'Drowned World' and how she traded love for fame, and how she doesn't need anybody to say "I love you, Madonna," except for those that truly know her and love her.

Favourite outfits A Seventies look when she was on the cover of Harper's Bazaar. The colours are beautiful, and she looks very simple, yet totally elegant and sexy.

Favourite Madonna moment Whatever she is experiencing right now, every moment, because this is truly her.

What's special about Madonna Her determination and courage to experiment and embrace new ideas into her work. Her voice – it's so unique and comes from a very deep place within her. Her attitude that embraces improving herself and not relying on others to get what she wants. Not being afraid to be powerful and vulnerable at the same time. Her demanding presence onstage. Her appreciation for family. Her toned body. Her continuing struggle to find a "deeper meaning for life". She doesn't care what her fans think. When she makes music and art, she's doing it for herself, but this is what caused one to be a true fan because you know it is truly from her heart and soul.

Inspiration She inspires me to pursue my goals and dreams, whatever they may be. She also influenced my extreme appreciation for music, of all genres and styles. She also inspires me to make an unremovable impression on this world... and to dance!

"*It was my destiny*

The kids of America were into hip hop, and had seized the term R&B from the dwindling gangs of greasers hawking their retro bump and grind around bars and bikers' clubs.

Madonna obviously wanted a piece of the action. From her earliest incarnation, striking out with the hard beats of New York City, she had led from the frontline of club culture. First into the mainstream with the Vogueing phenomenon, moving onwards with the modern assimilations of 'Erotica' (complete with 'Did You Do It''s wicked spoof on rap lyrics), she had no intention of growing old gracefully, resting on her laurels or simply disappearing, like so many of her former contemporaries. She had a good look around the block for hip, young producers to collaborate on her next album, *Bedtime Stories*, released in October 1994, and she handpicked four: Kenny "Babyface" Edmonds, Nellee Hooper, Dallas Austin and Dave "Jam" Hall.

Like *Erotica*, it was released on Madonna's own imprint, Maverick. Set up with a $60 million investment by Warner Bros, Madonna continues to run it not as a mere vanity label but as a fully-functioning business empire, with other signed artists including Alanis Morissette.

Bedtime Stories, like its predecessor, made a significant impression on the cool, club audiences for whom Madonna issued remixes of her tracks. Crucially, she remained a credible artist.

But she was at a crossroads visually. The videos she released from *Bedtime Stories* found Madonna looking backwards as well as forwards, some might say playing for time. For the hit single 'Secret', showing off her sparkling nose stud, she is Marilyn plus ten. With her hair short and blonde and her shiny, dark eye make-up just that bit overdone, Madonna also sports a Marie Antoinette beauty mark under her left eye, as she did for the MTV performance of 'Vogue'.

The clip typically shuffles two or three different scenarios. In one, Madonna's in a nightclub, fronting the sort of band you might expect to find blowing black jazz and blues in a Louisiana bar – except that she is singing the hauntingly delicious melodies of 'Secret', clad in a pencil skirt and a shiny top showing maximum cleavage, midriff and a crucifix. In other shots, she shimmers offstage in a halter-neck gown and stretches out in a bed as, again, she endorses inter-racial intimacy.

The promo for 'Bedtime Story' – co-written by Nellee Hooper and the eccentric Icelandic songstress Björk – is more diverse, a surreal dream sequence arising from some sort of controlled experiment on a prostrate Madonna, wearing a particularly unattractive combination of pale-blue eyeshadow and frosted peach lipstick.

Doves fly out of her belly, her eye turns into a mouth and sings, and her blonde hair juts out in knotty tufts as she poses in front of a giant sunflower. More beautiful in a billowing ballgown with long, fluffy hair falling round her shoulders, more striking as a black-haired animation with hostile make-up, more intriguing in a bouffant, 17th Century wig, or a long,

With one of her more unusual accessories (below), a chihuahua named Chiquita who enjoyed a starring role in Madonna's 1995 'Human Nature' video.

pale robe with a frilled neckline, she doesn't really have to fall back on that old standby, nudity, but she gets them out one more time to immerse herself in water, and she flashes up a sign to underline the message of the song: "Words are useless especially sentences."

Words, however, are her weapon in 'Human Nature'. Clearly using the song to lash out at the outcry over *Sex*, the fact that 'Erotica' was substantially overlooked and the backlash over her robustly sexual performances in *Body Of Evidence* and *Dangerous Game*, she returns to a familiar preoccupation with the hookline: "Express yourself, don't repress yourself."

"You wouldn't let me say the words I longed to say," she accuses. "You didn't want to see life through my eyes." Further along, she snaps: "Did I say something wrong? Oops, I didn't know I couldn't talk about sex," and looking straight into the camera at the end of the video, she promises, "Absolutely no regrets."

To stretch the point and to produce an irony, a humorous retort rather than an invitation to hardcore bondage games, she makes full use of an array of ropes and chains, filming the entire clip in a black, PVC catsuit while masked dancers writhe around in S&M costumes and Madonna's own chihuahua dog, Chiquita, makes its video debut.

Interestingly, Madonna finally gets to have a hairdo like those of the coloured girls she tried so hard to copy in her Michigan childhood. Very dark and braided into perfect lines, it's matched by the devilish blackness of her lipstick.

But of all of the videos released from the album, the most important was 'Take A Bow', its significance stretching far beyond the chorus of protest at its bullfighting content and suggestions of violence against women. Reviving her Spanish fascinations and co-starring with real-life bullfighter Emilio Munoz, Madonna comes on like a Bardot-esque sex kitten, wriggling around the home in her underwear with pouting red lips, her hair free and golden, parted in the middle, and her eyeliner applied with a dramatic and flattering sweep. More formally attired at the bullfight, she is aloof, elegant, with a tailored, tight-waisted Forties suit designed by John Galliano, long black gloves, her hair scraped back under a hat with a veil and the eyeliner heavily caked around her lids.

The video seemed to equate the death of the bull with a brutal sexuality, and Madonna was later criticised for her treatment of a sensitive subject. That was probably why she filmed a sequel for the video accompanying 'You'll See', giving her the opportunity to dump the swine in full view of the world.

It wasn't the bullfight or the punch-up that interested film director Alan Parker when he watched the 'Take A Bow' video. It was Madonna's ability to carry off the Forties look so graciously. Parker was casting *Evita*. He had been planning to make a film version of the Andrew Lloyd Webber/Tim Rice musical for years, and there had been huge competition for the part of Eva Peron between America's leading female singers and actresses. Names such as Meryl Streep, Barbra Streisand, *'to play this part'*

Liza Minnelli, Glenn Close and Bette Midler hurried in and out of the gossip columns before it was generally understood that Michelle Pfeiffer had won the part.

When Madonna heard that Pfeiffer had dropped out after having a baby, she launched a whole-hearted campaign on her own behalf, hand-writing a four-page letter to Parker in which she explained that she could bring to Peron to life like no one else – "... that only I could understand her passion and her pain".

She felt a huge affinity with the wife of the Argentinian President, not least because Peron's ambitious rise from rags to riches, using men along the way, echoed her own. Both, at the pinnacle of their fame, were surrounded by controversy, but campaigned for others. Madonna, thirty-seven when filming began, was just a few years older than Peron had been when she died from cancer in 1952. And at five feet four, she was a mere inch shorter than her character.

"It was my destiny to play this part," said Madonna later. "I knew this was the role of a lifetime – and I still believe it is."

It was not without some reservations that Parker and Lloyd-Webber agreed to hire her. Neither was completely convinced that her voice would rise to the challenge. Her acting abilities were also dubious, with Madonna having

suffered several flop movies and critical maulings. However, Parker and Lloyd-Webber were persuaded by Madonna's forceful enthusiasm and earnest promises.

She was as good as her word. She made her preparations as thoroughly as she had entered into everything else in her life that she'd set her heart on, taking vocal lessons from a coach in New York. "I found range and parts of my voice that I never knew I had," she recalled.

She also took an active part in selecting her costumes, working with the couture department as they sought out an authentic wardrobe. Costume designer Penny Rose found some of the clothes in vintage shops and costume-hire houses, and made copies of the Christian Dior gowns Eva Peron had worn. "Madonna was very interested in what she was wearing," said Penny. "It was a collaboration. Her input was pretty impressive."

She worked out every day to keep herself in tip-top condition for the movie, and she made it to her business to meet and learn from people who had known Eva Peron. In a major coup, she personally charmed Carlos Menem, the President of Argentina, into allowing her to film 'Don't Cry For Me, Argentina' on the actual balcony of the presidential palace, Casa Rosada – a request that had earlier been refused.

Madonna on the balcony of the Casa Rosada for *Evita*. After being refused permission to film on the actual premises, Madonna personally met with Argentinian President Carlos Menem who gave the shoot the green flag.

The Luvvies

Alan Parker (right), director of *Evita*: "I think that no one could have done it better than she did it. The only problem that ever came into my head was the fact that the icon, the celebrity, might get in the way. She's Madonna, she's as famous as Eva Peron was. So that's the only difficulty, the baggage that came with it, but I think she's transformed that."

Mike Myers, comedy actor and co-star in the *Beautiful Stranger* video:
Mike Myers: "Do you want to come over today?"
Madonna: "I'm getting my nails done. Maybe I'll drive down. Could I bring my girlfriend Ingrid?"

George Harrison (right), former Beatle, owner of HandMade Films producing *Shanghai Surprise*: "We had the wrong script, the wrong director and the wrong stars... The Beatles always handled the press brilliantly, and we had far more press than any pop star today. We also had a sense of humour about it."

Antonio Banderas (below), narrator in *Evita*: "I feel proud that I worked with Madonna at this particular time of her life. In a way, I thought always

while we were shooting the movie that *Evita*, the whole project and the character, specifically was for Madonna. I think she had to bring truth to the table to play this character, and she did it – otherwise it would have been impossible. I really like her; I have to defend her completely."

John Schlesinger (left), director of *The Next Best Thing*: "She was concerned about giving an able performance and a real truthful one, so she wasn't concerned about creating a persona that was anything to do with Madonna, just the person that she was playing in the movie."

Russell Lome, co-star of *A Certain Sacrifice*: "She had already adopted the practice of using one name, thinking of how the great stars of yesterday would become known by a single name at the height of their fame – Marilyn, Dietrich, Gable, Garbo, Liz, Brando. I guess Madonna wanted her name added to the list of one-name legends."

Ron Silver, co-star in the stage play *Speed The Plow* (right): "Most of the audience was there to see her. But I was thrilled. Here I was with a wonderful part in a wonderful play, and all this attention was being focused on the play because of Madonna."

Susan Seidelman, director of *Desperately Seeking Susan*: "Anyone who can break barriers, be outrageous, and bounce back up with grace, that's glamour. Madonna has always had an amazing sense of self... She has the kind of face you want to look at blown up fifty feet high. She isn't conventionally beautiful but then neither were the Bette Davises or Marlene Dietrichs."

Madonna on William Dafoe (*Body Of Evidence* co-star, left): "Gracious as a man, generous as an actor and absolutely the best pretend fuck I ever had."

EVITA

the dark-red dress, straight out of the Forties, was a glorious rose garden come to life

Madonna continued to play the role of *Evita* at international premieres by dressing in outfits that would not have looked amiss in the Forties. Madonna arrives (this page) at the London premiere dressed in green, a stark contrast to the fabulously over the top creation she wore (opposite) to the LA premiere .

Recording the vocal track in London and filming in Buenos Aires, Hungary and London, Madonna stopped off briefly in January 1996 to testify in a Los Angeles court against Robert Hoskins, a man who had been stalking her. He was sentenced to ten years' imprisonment. Madonna arrived dressed conservatively in a double-breasted suit, with her chestnut-coloured hair neatly fastened at the back.

In what may have been a response to the sexual availability that had long been an implication in her image – at least to some – the deranged Hoskins was under the delusion that they were married. He had broken into the grounds of her house in LA more than once, forcing Madonna to up sticks and run to her Miami home. In the final intrusion, one of Madonna's security guards shot Hoskins three times.

In every way, Evita came along at exactly the right time, although, rumour had it, actress Melanie Griffith wasn't too happy. Her husband had been cast as the narrator – and Madonna had made her attraction to Antonio Banderos crystal clear in In Bed With Madonna. Melanie was present during the filming, and insiders have gossiped that there was no love lost between the two women.

But a new and complicating set of circumstances arose during shooting, for which the producers had to make some urgent changes to the schedule: Madonna was pregnant. Declaring her scenes a priority, they managed to complete the film without the swelling Ciccone bump disrupting continuity, while their star dropped the more rigorous activities from her exercise routine, consulted with doctors and fought the sickness brought on by pregnancy in tandem with the exhaustion, stress and heat of the filming.

Ever the trouper, Madonna carried on through thick and thin. She replicated the dark looks of Peron by wearing brown lenses and wigs, thirty-nine different hats, forty-nine hairstyles and eighty-five costumes ranging from peasant dresses to shapely suits such as the one she had worn in 'Take A Bow', her dress becoming more glamorous and her jewellery more flamboyant as her character assumed more wealth and power.

Dior's outlines had looked revolutionary in the years after the Second World War. They featured a pulled-in waist, a full skirt and natural shoulders, often with a curvy peplum jacket, seamed stockings, gloves, boxed handbags and multiple strands of pearls. Tango dresses, with ruffles or polka dresses, were another post-War attraction.

The woman's hair was usually pulled back, and the make-up was pale with little cheek shading, a strong brow arch, thinly applied brown eyeliner, minimal mascara and red lipstick. Madonna liked Christian Dior's Indian Red, and Estee Lauder subsequently launched an Evita line.

The film premiered in December 1996 at the LA Shrine Auditorium. And if Madonna had looked beautiful in the period gowns she wore on the silver screen, she looked absolutely breathtaking in the creation she showed off at the premiere. It had been widely speculated that she would mark the occasion in Dolce & Gabbana. Since the birth of her daughter Lourdes in

October, she had made a string of public appearances in the Italian duo's coat-dresses and pants, taking on something of the look of a young Sophia Loren. Other experts pointed to her long associations with Jean Paul Gaultier, for whom she had modelled on the catwalk. She was known as a fan of Chanel and Gucci, and she had posed in fashion advertisements for Versace.

In the event, she made her entrance in a evening gown designed by John Galliano for Givenchy Couture. Living up to his reputation for "romantic, eccentric" garments, the dark-red dress, straight out of the Forties, was a glorious rose garden come to life, its plunging neckline adorned with hundreds of scraps of material, shaped and dyed and puckered to fashion a riot of petals and leaves. She accessorised with a matching "Miss Kitty" hat and veil, a co-ordinated lipstick shade and fabulous diamond earrings, her eyelids simply but affectingly stroked with liner, and her bottom lashes lightly brushed with mascara.

The screening was a resounding success, as was the film when it went on general release, grossing $160m at the box office. It won Madonna the sort of accolades she'd dreamed of all her life: her mastery of a complex vocal task was warmly applauded, the soundtrack album sold millions, and in her most rewarding moment, she won a Golden Globe award for Best Actress In A Musical Or Comedy.

For a new mother, Madonna was in amazing shape in January 1997, attending NBC's awards ceremony in a sophisticated revision of underwear as outerwear, her little black dress incorporating a daringly low-cut bra-top and a clinging skirt, teamed with the long gloves that had always been among her favourite fashion items. (Indeed, there is a website devoted entirely to Madonna's gloves.)

Her hair, parted slightly to the left, was blonde and natural, falling past her shoulders to soft flicks of curl at the ends. The lipstick was red but not garish, the eyebrows were gently coloured and naturally shaped, and the smoky shadow and liner accentuated her eyes without dominating her face. Accompanied by her baby's father, Carlos Leon, she looked happy, healthy and, as usual, porcelain-white.

"This is the role I was born to play," she said later of *Evita*. "I put everything of me into this because I was playing a woman so much like me. I was emotionally and physically exhausted, and sick from being pregnant. But I am prouder of *Evita* than anything else I have done."

She would later add:
"Besides my daughter."

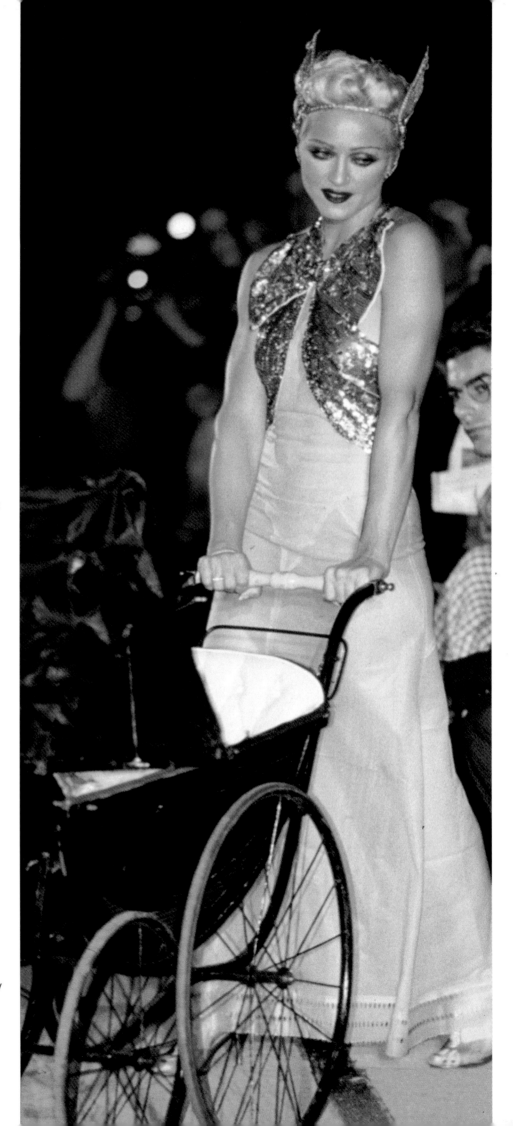

"Ever since my daughter was born, I feel the fleetingness of time...

Perhaps it was an irresistible urge, or a sudden impulse to return to the wild, old days before she got trapped by fame.

It certainly wasn't Madonna's style in 1994 to go picking up men in public parks, but by all accounts, this was how she met Carlos Leon. Out jogging in Central Park one autumn day, she spotted the future father of her child on a bicycle and approached him. Born in Manhattan, of Cuban-American heritage, Carlos was a personal fitness trainer working in a New York gym, with ambitions to be a world-class cyclist. He took Madonna for coffee and they began dating, on and off. She had long since split with Tony Ward, after, reportedly, enduring another abortion, for medical reasons.

At the time, Madonna was enjoying a fling with basketball star Dennis Rodman, but she soon sent him packing when she realized that he was indiscreet. He proved her right by selling to the newspapers saucy faxes he had received from Madonna, and by publishing a book in which he described and criticized their sex life.

Madonna then became closer to Carlos, who visited her in Buenos Aires during filming for *Evita*. There was much whispering at the time that Madonna's feelings for Carlos contained none of the passion she'd felt for Sean Penn, but she declared herself "deliriously happy" when she fell pregnant, allegedly by accident.

little more than a year, their spiritual adventures laid some foundations for the profound life changes that lay ahead for Madonna. "Yoga is very physical and strengthens me from within, not just externally," she enthused. "It helps me be more flexible about how I see the world and other people."

Madonna was becoming more flexible anyway. The birth of Lourdes had transformed her thinking – something which would become apparent in her attitude, her music and her appearance. She commented: "Ever since my daughter was born, I feel the fleetingness of time. And I don't want to waste it on getting the perfect lip colour."

Madonna surrendered the fanatical control she had always exerted over every aspect of her career to devote more time to Lourdes, and apparently repaired her relationship with her father and stepmother during their first visit to meet the baby.

There were shades of Tony Ciccone's strict parenting in the way Madonna would raise Lourdes, restricting her exposure to television and undesirable adult influences, vowing to teach her the importance of real relationships rather than online communication, and insisting on the importance of education, wishing for a world in which "schoolteachers would be paid more than movie stars and basketball players".

Appearing on German TV show *Wetten Das* in February '98, Madonna relaxes (opposite) while a video is played by flipping through the *Vanity Fair* pictorial of herself and Lourdes. She seems truly relaxed for a rare moment.

...and I don't want to waste it on getting the perfect lip colour"

Replying to suggestions that she had used Carlos as a "stud service", Madonna retorted: "I realize these comments are all made by persons who cannot live with the idea that something good is happening to me."

However, she didn't seem that keen on getting married, and furiously objected to a school of opinion which condemned her for setting fans a bad example with her intention to be a single mother.

Only months after the birth by Caesarian section of Lourdes Maria Ciccone Leon on 14 October, 1996, in LA, the relationship between Madonna and Carlos was over, and he signed over sole custody of the child – although he still sees his daughter regularly, and speaks with the highest regard for Madonna as a mother.

In 1997, another love interest came along in the shape of English actor and TV writer Andy Bird, who was ten years her junior. They shuttled between a house in London's Chelsea and Madonna's home in LA, and shared her recent interest in the ancient, mystical philosophy of Kabbalah, "marrying" in a ritual at which Madonna, reportedly, sported a long, white dress and bare feet.

Madonna and Bird took yoga lessons at a centre in north west London, and although the affair would run out of steam in

Madonna has also been stern about junk food, and reportedly keeps sweet Pop Tarts out of Lourdes' reach.

Most surprisingly, Madonna has introduced her daughter to Catholicism, having had her christened in Miami. The woman who had outraged the Christian world with "blasphemous" imagery said: "I want my daughter to read The Bible. But I will also explain to her that these are stories that people made up to teach people. This is not, like, the rule."

On another occasion, she declared: "Say what you will about Catholicism, the things you pick up along the way do help you by giving you something to turn to when you're in trouble. Then, when you have that foundation, you can start looking at other philosophies – which is what I've done."

She further explained: "There are indisputable truths that connect all religions, and I find that very comforting. My spiritual journey is to be open to everything. I believe that God is in all of us and that we are all capable of being gods and goddesses. That's my brand of Catholic mysticism. Throw some Buddhism in there and you've got my religion."

There are some who would say that Madonna had reinvented herself as a hippie. She let her hair grow into a long, untamed tangle coloured warm shades of honey-blonde and auburn. She rediscovered denim, and dressed in saris for

Attending the 1998 Oscars, Madonna continued to look every inch the pre-Raphaelite heroine, clothed and made-up with subtle hues of violet and pale pink.

The Men

Madonna: "I've never gotten to a point where there's been no man. But I've certainly had my moments where I've thrown up my hands and said, 'Ugh, men! They're just so endlessly disappointing.'"

According to Madonna as she searched for that perfect person, caring and sharing, smartness, sensitivity, sexiness and "a good body" were "extremely important". If he was a good dancer and dressed well, that was "an added plus". Wealth wasn't important "as long as he can pay his own rent". A fancy car was desirable, "as long as it's clean with a good stereo". Height and looks were of no importance.

Eventually, Madonna met her match in Guy Ritchie. Before that, she enjoyed some famous liaisons.

Steve Bray

Madonna met Steve Bray while attending the University Of Michigan in 1976. A drummer in a local band, he became first her lover and then one of her most important collaborators.

Bray: "If people feel exploited by Madonna, that's resentment of someone who's got drive."

Madonna: "He was the first guy I ever allowed to buy me a drink. He was irresistibly handsome."

Dan Gilroy

In the spring of 1979, Madonna met Dan at a party, and joined The Breakfast Club – the band he had with his brother Ed.

Gilroy: "I remember the very first time I met her at this party, she was wearing a kind of circus outfit... very short with a tutu and leggings a darker shade of blue than her tutu. Sure she had incredible style. Absolutely. And she had olive oil in her hair which made it quite strange and matted and those were the kinds of things people were doing then. It was definitely influenced by punk, but you could see she was moving in her own direction."

Mark Kamins

Kamins was a hot DJ at the trendy Danceteria club in New York when Madonna sought him out as a boyfriend in 1981.

Kamins: "She used her sexuality as a performer, but it's also how she got over offstage. We started hot, and it just got hotter... Madonna manipulates in her own way but I don't think there's a mean bone in her body... maybe a knuckle or two."

Jellybean Benitez

The next year saw Madonna hitching up with acclaimed DJ and remixer Jellybean, who gave her the chance to learn first-hand about the music industry.

Jellybean to author J Randy Taraborrelli: "For about a year and a half, I loved her very much. She was everything to me, my woman, my favourite artist, the bitchiest, funniest, smartass I had ever known. Yes, she used me to 'network' into the business. But I did the same for her.

"I think one of the biggest misconceptions is that the people Madonna used along the way didn't also get something out of the deal for themselves. But just by being associated with her, if you played your cards right, you could advance your career. Her position was that if you could get something out of exploiting her, the way she would you, then go for it."

Prince

Madonna began dating Prince in 1985 after meeting the strange and shy star at the American Music Awards. It wasn't a match made in heaven, although she has one pleasant and enduring memory.

Madonna: "Ever since I've known Prince I've attached a smell to him, which is lavender, and I don't know why. He reeks of it... he's very private and very shy. He's great when you get to know him, charming and funny in his own way. More than anything, he really comes alive when he's working... I think Prince leads a very isolated life and I don't... and that is the big difference between us."

Sean Penn

On one of their first dates, Madonna and Penn visited Marilyn Monroe's crypt. They married, after something of a whirlwind romance, in August 1985 and were divorced four years later.

Penn: "She's the most wonderful woman. I love her."

Madonna: "I think he's an incredible actor and I think he's done very well and I'm honoured to know him. He's an incredible human being. He's intelligent, he's talented and even though things didn't work out for us in terms of our marriage, I don't regret marrying him for a moment."

Sean: "I admit it, I was a smartass. And so was she. It was a relationship made in heaven, two smartasses going through life together. How romantic."

Madonna: "I felt that no one wanted us to be together. They celebrated our union, and then they wanted us to be apart. There were rumours about us getting a divorce a week after the wedding."

John Kennedy Jr

Madonna was allegedly romancing the former President's son during the death throes of her marriage to Penn. As an admirer of Monroe, she was thrilled to be dating someone whose father had enjoyed an affair with the tragic actress. However, the formidable Jackie Kennedy was horrified that her son should be mixed up with the controversial Madonna and refused to give her blessing to the friendship. Kennedy, allegedly a bit of a mummy's boy, caved in to the pressure.

Warren Beatty

Warren was allegedly another of Madonna's extra-marital interests, and the pair made it official when she split with Sean Penn in 1989. There was a great deal of suspicion about the nature of Madonna's relationship with the legendary womaniser. Some thought it was a publicity stunt for *Dick Tracy*, while others thought Beatty was a career move into the movies for Madonna.

Vanilla Ice

Madonna spent much of 1992 in the company of the rap star with the chiselled cheekbones. In musical circles, he was a laughing stock; hardly your genuine gangsta rapper.

Ice: "She's very sexy, she's hot, she's romantic. She's got a great body for her age." (Madonna was thirty-five at the time)

Dennis Rodman

In 1994, Madonna had a short fling with the bad-boy basketball star, and it was one she would regret. He sold a series of sexy faxes that he had received from Madonna, and he published a book in which he was uncomplimentary about their bedroom exploits.

Carlos Leon

The personal trainer and aspiring professional cyclist has a tattoo on his arm reading "September 8 forever". It was the day in 1994 that his life changed: the day he met Madonna in New York's Central Park. Two years later, she gave birth to his daughter, Lourdes.

Madonna: "I was madly in love with him, and it's a ludicrous accusation (that she used him as a 'sperm donor'). I don't know where it came from. It's not fair. It's not fair to me and it's not fair to him... He's an excellent father."

Leon: "All I can say is, it's great being a dad."

Andy Bird

After parting from Carlos shortly after Lourdes' birth, Madonna met English actor and TV writer Andy Bird in 1997. Despite finding much in common, including the Kabbalah, their relationship crumbled amid rumours that Andy was proving too laid-back for the driven and ambitious Madonna. She was still with Andy when she met Guy Ritchie chez Sting and Trudie Styler in the summer of 1998.

Guy Ritchie

Madonna: "It only took me forty years to find my soulmate!"

"I'm *slowly* revealing *myself,* my true *nature*"

Rolling Stone, taking her influence from paintings of Krishna. She somehow mislaid her famous beauty spot. She cleared out her make-up bag and showed a natural face touched with a little eye shadow and mascara, and lipstick in warm shades of pink and cherry. She added to her jewellery with the sort of necklaces you'd find at a street market along with joss sticks and bottles of essential oils. She gave up her rigorous exercise routines in favour of yoga.

The combination of motherhood and New Age possibility wrought dramatic changes as she wove her fascinations into her next album, *Ray Of Light*. Even more surprisingly, these elements mixed harmoniously with the forward-looking structures of the music.

Madonna had completed her explorations of American street culture with *Erotica* and *Bedtime Stories*. Those albums had been well-received by critics and fans who looked to Madonna for intelligent and creative pop, but with sales of five and six million respectively, they had fallen short of the commercial triumphs of *Like A Virgin* and *True Blue* which had clocked up nineteen million each, or Like A Prayer (thirteen million). The *Evita* soundtrack had restored Madonna's fortunes with more than eleven million copies crossing the counter. She wanted to match it with a project of her own, and she succeeded with *Ray Of Light*, released in March 1998.

Looking to trip hop and the chilled-out beats that had been sweeping Europe, she recruited renowned producer William Orbit, with his team, and her old collaborator Patrick Leonard. Within a new, updated and wholly persuasive musical environment, she renounced the idea that fame equals happiness, quoted yogic teachings, vowed to follow a more enlightened path through life, praised the healing powers of water, hoped for true love and waved goodbye forever to the old, shockaholic Madonna. This year's model was considered, compassionate, maternal, a friend of the earth and a student of the great beyond.

"Love is all we need," she cries in 'Nothing Really Matters', echoing The Beatles' Sixties' idealism. "Looking at my life/It's very clear to me/I lived so selfishly..." she confesses.

She later commented: "There is a trance-y, dreamy quality to a lot of the production, and if that is how people define New Age, then that's fine. But I never think of New Age music as having a point of view. I think it's meant to create the effect of you not thinking of anything in particular, and the last thing I want to do is to make a record that makes people not think."

Whether they were thinking or not, they bought the album – despite the critics' scepticism – and it went on to top the chart in forty different countries.

The videos from *Ray Of Light* were not consistently illuminating. In the mysterious wastelands of 'Frozen', the brooding farewells of 'The Power Of Goodbye' and the Japanese-style nightmare fantasy of 'Nothing Really Matters', Madonna aims for style above substance, darkness over light.

Her hair is raven, her clothes are black, apart from a red kimono outfit in 'Nothing Really Matters', and her atmospheres are powerful and disturbing. She does, however, hint at personal developments with her henna-painted hands in 'Frozen'.

By contrast, 'Ray Of Light' and 'Drowned World', are bright, celebratory, ringing out loud and clear what is really happening with Madonna. She has said: "I think 'Ray Of Light' is one of my greatest songs," adding: "(It) is about how small I feel in the big picture – but then how big everything feels too, and how life seems to be going by faster than the speed of light and yet if you get outside of yourself and become your own witness, you can also stop it."

Accordingly, the video whizzes along at a tremendous pace, the images of commuters in their daily grind flash-forwarding past while Madonna sings and dances uninhibitedly under a blue sky, a sunset and the strobe lights of a disco. She is radiant, happy, at peace with the world with her flyaway hair, her denim jacket, her jeans with the sparkly belt and her famous tummy bared to the elements.

'Drowned World/Substitute For Love' is entirely autobiographical, reconstructing scenes in which Madonna struggles through crowds of lightbulb-popping pressmen and monstrous strangers at showbiz parties. "I find I've changed my mind... this is my religion!" she sings, closing her front door and clasping a little girl tight to her heart.

Asked about her latest incarnation, Madonna rejected the theory of reinvention. "I'm slowly revealing myself, my true nature," she said. "It feels to me like I'm just getting closer to the core of who I really am."

Part of that true nature was a sense of humour which, Madonna believed, her critics had consistently overlooked. Contributing 'Beautiful Stranger', a William Orbit co-write, to the movie, *Austin Powers: The Spy Who Shagged Me*, Madonna filmed a hilarious, Sixties' Bond spoof sequence with comic actor Mike Myers.

Dressed in a black, glittery, strappy top with her bra showing, calf-length pants and stilettoes, she entrances the geeky Powers who is in a disco, watching her dance on the stage. It's a joyous, carefree, arms-flinging dance, maybe like the ones she performed all those years ago in the school disco, and her leather-jacketed advances to Powers in a car afterwards recall and lampoon all the awkward encounters of the classic American teenager.

To seal her recent happiness and success, Madonna won three Grammys for *Ray Of Light* at the 1999 ceremony at the LA Shrine Auditorium. She was honoured for Best Pop Album, Best Dance Recording and Best Short Form Music Video, and she performed 'Nothing Really Matters' in a red kimono like the one in the promo clip, black-haired and made up to look Japanese.

The next year, with 'Beautiful Stranger', she took another Grammy: Best Song Written For A Motion Picture.

It seemed like things couldn't get better, but they did.

In recent years Madonna has experimented with trends from many different cultures, more often than not with great success. At the VH-1 Fashion Awards in October 1998 (above), Madonna appeared as a Gothic heroine straight out of Dracula. Madonna's first attempt at Indian chic dated from the April 1994, when she had her nose and belly button pierced (inset). February 1999 (opposite) saw the star unveil a new Geisha-inspired look for the 'Nothing Really Matters' video and a live appearance at the Grammies.

"I feel like he's my equal and that's hard to find. He makes me laugh, he's gorgeous, he's brilliant and we're very much in love"

Back in New York at the turn of the Eighties, playing Police covers with her band Emmy, Madonna could never have dreamed that she would one day share a dinner table with their blond singer and songwriter Sting.

But by the time the Nineties were drawing to an end, she numbered Sting and his wife Trudie Styler among her closest friends. Staying at their country home in Wiltshire for a party in the summer of 1998, she was captivated by the young film-maker Guy Ritchie, director of the British smash-hit *Lock, Stock & Two Smoking Barrels*.

Ritchie, ten years her junior, was born into a well-to-do family in Hatfield, Herts, although his parents' marriage broke up when he was still in short trousers. He grew up with the hunting, fishing, shooting set, but cultivated an image as a bit of a Cockney tough guy with a colourful street experience. Indeed, he travelled and took menial jobs before breaking into the music business, making videos for bands. In Madonna's first impressions, "I knew that he was a formidable human being and a great talent with a brilliant mind."

There were rumours that at the time, Madonna enjoyed a short romance with the charming and resolutely macho Ritchie, who once declared, "There's something honest about violence. Some things are just better settled there and then."

They spent months on opposite sides of the Atlantic, with Madonna in America, keeping in touch by letter. She broke up her relationship with Andy Bird, while Guy split with his girlfriend Rebecca Green, TV presenter and daughter of Carlton television boss Michael Green.

By the beginning of 1999, Madonna and Guy were back together, exuding an easy familiarity in which Ritchie would soon enjoy the rare privilege of being allowed to prick the royal bubble. Undaunted by her immense celebrity, he calls her Madge and "the missus", and his well-mannered, down-to-earth personality appears to temper some of her more extravagant instincts.

She would later say: "I feel like he's my equal and that's hard to find. He makes me laugh, he's gorgeous, he's brilliant and we're very much in love." She also adored "his super-macho ways".

Madonna's home life was now as fulfilling as her spiritual endeavour and her most recent achievements in music and the movies. In buoyant mood, she began work on her next album, *Music*, again with William Orbit and a new collaborator, French writer and producer Mirwais, who had sent a tape to Maverick.

The sessions began in the autumn of 1999, continuing into the new Millennium in LA, New York and London, where Madonna now cut a familiar figure. There was a whirl of publicity insisting that Madonna had become an Anglophile. Certainly, she was quick with comments such as "I'm having a love affair with England." She was househunting in London, she was seen drinking pints of Guinness in pubs, she was affecting an amusing, clipped, English accent, she was picking up the native slang and she was building a circle of friends that included Sir Paul McCartney's daughter Stella – who was a hot

property in international fashion circles for the sexy, feminine and thoroughly modern clothes she was designing for Chloe.

But for all of Madonna's frequently professed fondness for London, the taxis, the antique shops and the monarchy, it was originally more for Guy Ritchie's sake than her own that she visited so often. She said: "It was an, 'OK, I don't want to move to England,' 'Well, I don't want to move to America,' type of thing. Of course, being the girl, I made the first compromise... I picked up my life and my daughter and everything and I rented a house in London, and moved there... And that's really when our relationship started to work. But it was a huge sacrifice for me... "

She recalled in a later interview: "Everyone thinks and writes that I've become a complete Anglophile. They say I've got no interest in America. But that's so not true. In fact, sometimes you have to go away from something to really appreciate and see it."

The songs on *Music* had been inspired by America, or at least a particular period in its history. Madonna stated: "I just love the whole iconography of the West – the kind of sturdy earthiness of it, the earthy, rural part. But it's got to have an edge to it too. I think there's something really folky about a lot of the stuff that I wrote. It's really simple and lyrical, but then you combine it with modern technology."

Guy was working with Brad Pitt on his second film, Snatch, and it was during this period that Madonna became pregnant again. Overjoyed to be expecting another child, she shrugged off the negative and often nasty reviews she received in March 2000 for her latest movie venture, a co-starring role with Rupert Everett in a gay-themed romantic comedy called *The Next Best Thing*.

Announcing their happy news in a joint statement, Madonna and Guy awaited the birth at their home in LA, where she wore second-time-around maternity wear designed by the likes of Abe Hamilton.

During her "confinement", Madonna managed to offend all of England by declaring in a radio interview that she would not be keen to have her baby in a UK hospital since they were "old and Victorian". She added: "I like efficiency."

As it turned out, she needed fast and efficient treatment when she ran into trouble a couple of weeks before the estimated day of arrival. Madonna had already been diagnosed with an abnormal condition of the placenta, and she raced to hospital at the first signs of discomfort. Rocco was born by Caesarian section in the early hours of 11 August. It was a difficult surgery, with Madonna losing a large amount of blood, and her son was kept in intensive care for several days until his lungs had become slightly more developed and his jaundice treated.

The birth of Rocco cemented the bonds between Madonna and her father.

Tony Ciccone has talked publicly of his pride in his daughter, often with the odd crack at his own or Madonna's expense: "Sometimes I think I'm better as a grandfather than I

At the premiere (opposite) of Guy Ritchie's *Snatch*, Madonna wore a classic white Chloe suit. Stylish from the front, the back of the jacket was adorned with the legend, 'Mrs Ritchie'. Stepping out (below) in London, a pregnant Madonna looks divinely happy in the arms of her British husband.

Madonna and Child

Little Lourdes may not be allowed to watch much telly or eat her favourite Pop Tarts, but she's quite the young lady when it comes to style.

Lola, as she's known, is reported to have £35,000 worth of clothes in her wardrobe, with Madonna quoted as saying that she wants her daughter to be "the best-dressed girl in the world".

"She loves clothes, jewellery and dressing-up," added Madonna. "She's the girliest girl I know – next to me."

Even as a baby, Lourdes enjoyed the best of everything: an antique cot worth thousands, and Pratesi sheets costing £700.

She has inherited some of her mother's past and present tastes, with a liking for lacy clothes and leather jackets. One of her favourite kiddie labels is Bunny London, specialising in embroidered denim and Eastern-type frocks with fringes and floral patterns, and matching bags. She's a welcome customer, too, at the Kensington children's store What Katy Did.

A budding cyclist, like daddy, she's well provided with shorts, often teamed with a slogan T-shirt, and her sportswear also includes child-sized Maharishi pants.

Occasionally, mother and daughter are colour co-ordinated when they go out together, and the Caten twins made Lourdes a pair of Western-style, 'Drowned World' pants like Madonna's.

Lourdes is partial to a nice bit of jewellery, too. She's often seen with strings of beads, thin gold bracelets, earrings and a toe-ring. For special occasions, she has diamond and jewel-studded bracelets.

Accompanying Madonna to her favourite London hairdresser Daniel Galvin's salon recently, Lourdes was treated to a manicure and nail polish.

Like every little girl wanting to "dress up", Lourdes dabbles with make-up, and is the proud owner of some fun children's products from Miss Molly, bought by Madonna in Paris.

No child of a superstar can possibly get by without a decent pair of sunglasses, and Lourdes steps out in mini-aviators by Christian Dior, at £120 a pair.

At home, the dark-haired, dark-eyed Lola lives in style. Her bedroom reportedly features a £34,000, custom-weaved rug, and she sits on pink, silk-padded, limited-edition chairs costing £300 each.

She takes lessons in French and art, and is learning karate.

Like Lourdes, her little brother Rocco has travelled the world in a private jet and gleaming limousines, stays in the finest hotels and has his dinner in the finest restaurants.

He was christened in a Donatella Versace gown and he wore a kilt in the Ritchie family's Hunting Mackintosh tartan to match his dad's at his wedding to Madonna.

Although Rocco's personal tastes in clothes have yet to develop, he's been snapped in expensive romper suits, fleeces, shirts, T-shirts, tank tops, pants, camouflage gear, waterproof jackets, checks, stripes, elastic belts, scarves, hats and tiny trainers.

He sees the world from a traditional, four-wheeled pushchair or, often, from his father's shoulders. Guy has been photographed around the world with the fair- and fluffy-haired Rocco, memorably in New York's Central Park in July 2001, where the eleven-month-old, in a blue-and-white striped all-in-one outfit with short sleeves and matching socks, showed off his new skill: walking.

It's believed that both children will be educated, at least in part, in exclusive British schools.

Lourdes Ciccone will be the most envied girl among schoolmates with her £35,000 wardrobe and diamond-studded bracelets. Often dressed to reflect her mother's look, she is pictured here in Indian garb (main picture) and (below) on a rare public family outing at Versailles.

2000 saw Madonna re-emerge with the acclaimed *Music* album and another startling image change. This time the look was pure rhinestone cowgirl, whether strumming a guitar on the 'Don't Tell Me' video shoot (opposite), posing at the MTV Europe Music Awards in November 2000 (below), or riding a mechanical bull for another photo shoot. At the album's LA launch party, she traded places with Guy, promoting his latest film with a slashed black T-shirt and allowing him to don a rhinestone-encrusted *Music* T-shirt with designer denim.

probably was at a father. But let's face it, Madonna was a special case. I think anyone would sympathise with the father who had the job of raising Madonna."

For her part, things fell into place when she became a parent herself. She stated: "I love my father... Anyone who knows me knows that I am my father. He's strict, like me. Loving, too, I hope like me. His work ethic is ingrained in me. Now that I have a family, I have so much respect for him and the way he tried to hold ours together, back when I was a bratty little kid... It's hard to see all of that until you have children."

Around the same time, Madonna enjoyed another successful birth – her 'Music' single. This followed the release of a bizarre cover version of the early Seventies' hit 'American Pie' by singer/songwriter Don McLean from the soundtrack of *The Next Big Thing*. It was a smash, but it confused her fans with its lyrical puzzles, it outraged the old longhairs who protested that the original was better, and it annoyed quite a few other people who wondered why she had bothered to revive such a preposterous old chestnut in the first place. McLean, however, was delighted. Asked what it meant to him, he replied: "It means I will never have to work again."

'Music' was a much fresher proposition. Her eagle eye trained as keenly as ever on current trends, she chose to work once again with a comedian for the promo video. This time, it was Britain's ultra-hip presenter Ali G, playing a limousine driver – number plates MUFF DADDY – to Madonna's playgirl, frolicking with a bevy of gal-pals in the interior. (They include two of her long-term, real-life friends, Debi Mazar and Niki Haris.)

Wrapped in white fake-fur, clanking with jewellery and swigging champagne, Madonna lives it up while her driver fails dismally to get a look in, either with the partying in the car or at the pole-dancing club. The ghetto-fabulous video, in part, sends up DJ culture, breaking into cartoon format briefly as Madonna takes over the booth for a bit of scratching. She was later said to have described Ali G as "brilliant" and "the Peter Sellers of our generation".

The real Madonna had not changed alarmingly. Her hair remained long and tangly, and her make-up emphasised pale pink lipstick and lots of dark lashes, but the most telling item was the stetson, the symbol of her latest theme.

The *Music* album was launched in September 2000 with a party for six hundred people at an old haunt of Madonna's, a black, gay club in LA. There, she greeted her guests in a black, customised T-shirt celebrating Guy's movie, Snatch. Guy returned the favour by wearing a red shirt promoting *Music*.

Contrary to popular opinion, Madonna did not create the T-shirt phenomenon – it had started in London – but, with her usual ability to spot a good thing, and her proven friendliness

"*…obviously I'm embracing it because I know it's going to confuse people…*"

towards message clothes over the years, she was the first to publicise it and set off a worldwide craze which would show no signs of abating for another year at least. Before long, every girl band, TV presenter, soap star and two-bit celebrity would be proclaiming something or other on a cut-up T-shirt.

The most famous of Madonna's shirts was the black one which immortalised the name of Britney Spears. She wore it several times on a short promotional tour for *Music*, memorably at a live show in New York and on the Letterman TV show in November 2000. Some felt that Madonna was being ironic, taking the mickey out of herself and Britney. Others felt that it was her way of communicating with a generation of young record-buyers.

Madonna herself told *Elle* magazine: "I love Britney… I became obsessed with wearing (Britney) T-shirts. I slept in them as well. It was like I felt it would bring me luck."

She elaborated to journalist Ingrid Sischy: "Well, obviously I'm embracing it because I know it's going to confuse people, but the true essence of my feelings for her is that I feel really protective of her. Don't even ask me why."

She displayed the words Kylie Minogue in gold and silver script on another black, customised T-shirt worn with violet, patterned pants, also in November, at the MTV Europe Awards in Stockholm, where she performed 'Music' and picked up trophies for Best Female and Best Dance.

In January 2001, Madonna expanded the concept to other clothes, appearing at the Hollywood premiere of Guy's *Snatch* movie in a white, Chloe trouser suit emblazoned on the back with her name in silver sequins: Mrs Ritchie. As a side effect, the outfit featured in a series of fashion articles hailing the return of the white suit.

Madonna celebrated herself again the next month, performing at the Grammy Awards in a black vest with Material Girl in large, silver lettering. She didn't win a Grammy, but she was awarded a Brit for Best International Female, also in February, and sent a humorous thank-you video in which she appeared in a dressing gown bearing the initials of Guy Ritchie.

Come March, she was photographed in a white, short-sleeved T-shirt bearing a Union Jack and the logo Uncle Jack. In July, the message on a light-coloured vest, teamed with jeans, was "Punk", and in a new fashion controversy, she wore her latest accessory – a silver mini-pistol – attached to her belt, along with a chain. Also in July, her tops declared, "You suck" and "London, juicy couture for nice girls." In August, she widened the brief again, stepping out with the legend Madge above her left breast on a zipped-up, hooded sports outfit.

Back in December 2000, as part of her promotional tour, Madonna had shown off yet another of her T-shirts in London, where she performed a private concert for fans and industry people in the "intimate" surroundings of the London Brixton Academy.

Her first UK appearance in seven years, it stirred enormous excitement, it was described by hardened music journalists as "the gig of the decade" and it was broadcast online to an audience of nine million through a deal with Microsoft. Madonna had been personally involved in setting up the internet project, showing her usual media savvy and her unflagging capacity for progress. Tickets for the concert changed hands for up to a thousand pounds each.

Madonna had arranged for Dolce & Gabbana to design her clothes and decorate the venue and the stage with a Western theme appropriate to her latest incarnation as a 21st Century cowgirl. The accommodating Italians provided golden haystacks, silver cacti, massive Ms at every turn and pink stetsons a-go-go.

And Madonna made an entrance to end them all – not on the main stage, but at the side wall where a Union Jack flag suddenly fell to reveal Madonna and her troupe, dancing wildly on top of a big, white Chevvy with a mirrorball hanging in the windscreen. The audience had no sooner caught its collective breath than she sailed right over their heads, crowd-surfing to the main stage for a set in which she avoided all of her golden oldies apart from 'Holiday'.

Flashing the names of her children in gold studs on the back and front of a comprehensively slashed, black T-shirt, and showing generous expanses of side, tummy and muscular arms, she completed the outfit with flared, hipster jeans in dark denim and a wide, gold belt.

Glitter and gold confetti fell from above as the show ended, and critics who had never particularly liked Madonna were already dribbling words like "blistering", "triumphant", "hot", "euphoric", "foxy" and "frenetic".

But she had more on her mind than the reviews. For all the hue and cry over the concert, there was something much bigger on the agenda for Madonna.

Not content with setting the prevailing cowboy trend, Madonna swiftly popularised 'ironic' custom T-shirts, promoting Kylie at the European MTV Awards in 2000 (opposite), new baby Rocco at her legendary November 2000 Brixton gig (below left) and, most surprisingly, her 1984 hit 'Material Girl' at the Grammies (below).

WhatMadonnaSaysAboutThem...

The Queen of Pop...

Madonna and Diana, Princess Of Wales, could have been great friends. They met once, and were planning another get-together before the fatal car smash in a tunnel in Paris.

On the face of it, they had a great deal in common. Both had grown up in public, weathering scandal, controversy and some fantastic fashion disasters to become leaders of style and role models to millions.

Both women were hounded by the paparazzi, and Madonna's portrayal of the car-chasing photographers in her video for 'Drowned World'/'Substitute For Love' brought criticism for its similarities to the scenes leading to Diana's death. "For a start, I have been chased through that same Paris underpass where the crash occurred, more times than I can count," said Madonna. "Anyone who has ever been chased like that and who has had to live that sort of life hit the wall with her. I think that both of our lives have been affected by fame, hers obviously more so than my own..."

Madonna had played the part of Diana in a comedy sketch opening the new season of American TV programme *Saturday Night Live* (above left and right) in 1985.

The pair met ten years later at a party in London, while Madonna was working on *Evita*, where they had a brief conversation about the problems of fame, but plans for Diana to visit were reportedly called off by Madonna after stalker Robert Hoskins was apprehended in the grounds of her LA home in 1995. Diana died in August 1997.

It was later confirmed by a spokesman for Althorp House, Diana's family home and her final resting place, that Madonna and Guy had inquired about the possibility of holding their wedding there – but the idea was called off by mutual agreement. Althorp's David Fawkes said: "It is not true to say Earl Spencer rejected the star, only that we could not provide the facilities."

...and the Princess

In The Wardrobe

ROB SEDUSKI *Chief Wardrobe Co-Ordinator since the "Who's That Girl?" tour*

"I work with Madonna and the designers to make sure all the costumes and accessories are reinforced, making them easy to get into and get out of. We're talking Velcro, snaps, snap tape, everything.

"We have four copies of each costume. We always have a second costume standing right next to the first so if there's a disaster, we'd substitute the double for the original. Like, within a split second. We haven't had to yet, thank God.

"The Geisha girl on the 'Drowned World' tour was the most difficult to get her in and out of. She has to first put on a pair of tights that we've cut the feet out of. And tights tend to roll and snag when they're put on too quickly... Then there's the red kimono worn underneath a harness. Then there's fingerless gloves with long sleeves attached. Then there's a wig. Then there's an over-kimono with long, black sleeves. That change, which is the second in the show, takes about five people to do in under three and a half minutes.

"She's very hands on. She directs the whole thing. I never had a problem with her. She's always been totally focused and easy to deal with. If you're straight ahead with her, she's fine. I love that she's always combined theatrics with fashion. That is something that she initiated. It's her trademark."

Rehearsing for the Drowned World Tour in early 2001, Madonna is seen here mastering the flying apparatus used for the 'Sky Fits Heaven' routine.

"It was **truly** a magical, religious experience – the whole week"

They went to Scotland to christen Rocco and get married.

Their guests were invited to stay for five days at the beautiful and remote Skibo Castle in the hills of Dornoch, Firth.

Guy booked all of the bedrooms on the estate for the duration of the celebrations, hired a team of seventy security guards and made every possible arrangement to protect the couple from media intrusion.

There was a star-studded guestlist, including family members from both sides and Carlos Leon, matchmakers Sting and Trudie, Madonna's close friend Gwyneth Paltrow, maid-of-honour Stella McCartney, Donatella Versace, Jean Paul Gaultier, Rupert Everett, Sacha Baron Cohen (Ali G), Jean Baptiste Mondino, actors Jason Statham and Jason Flemyng and the best men: Guy's producer Matthew Vaughn and London club owner Piers Adam.

Watched by hundreds of locals, the glitterati attended Rocco's christening at the 13th century cathedral in Dornoch, just a few miles away from the castle, on the evening of December 21.

Rocco was draped in a white gown embroidered with gold and designed by Donatella, while Madonna smiled broadly and happily for the sightseers and the cameras in a white, double-breasted Chloe coat, a black-veiled hat and long, sparkling earrings.

Unknown to Madonna and Guy, a man had sneaked into the cathedral twenty-four hours earlier and hidden behind an organ with food, drink and a bin-liner for use as a portable toilet. Robert Podesta, a fifty-two-year-old security adviser from Wales, filmed the whole ceremony, but was caught by guards on his way out and later fined a thousand pounds.

There would be no more intruders, and the royal couple would not be seen again until they left Scotland – with Dornoch reportedly two and a half million pounds the richer for their visit and the tourist industry hoping to capitalise on the publicity. "Follow Mad-donna and get married in bonny Scotland" cried one travel supplement.

The couple released no official photographs of their wedding on December 22. It's said that Madonna looked "like a princess" as she walked through the castle's Great Hall and up a red-carpeted staircase in her wedding dress, designed by Stella McCartney. The strapless creation, made of ivory silk, featured a fitted, corset-style bodice, a long train and an antique, lace veil. She added a garter, shoes by Jimmy Choo, a lily-of-the-valley bouquet and some very valuable pieces of jewellery.

They included a tiara encrusted with 767 diamonds, which she borrowed from Asprey & Garrard, a diamond cross custom-made by the House Of Harry Winston and three-inch-wide bracelets of diamonds and pearls from Adler. The ring that Guy slipped on to Madonna's finger as they stood at the top of the staircase was a comparatively modest platinum band, inset with a few small diamonds.

Prior to Madonna's grand entrance, the stairs had been scattered with rose petals by Lourdes, who wore a long, short-sleeved, high-necked dress, also in ivory and designed by Stella. Baby Rocco was kitted out in a green and navy kilt to match his dad's, and although it's been reported that Guy observed tradition by wearing nothing under his kilt, it's fair to assume that his son had to differ.

Madonna changed into yet another ivory-coloured McCartney outfit, this time a trouser suit, for the evening dance, "decked out in diamonds" lent by Harry Winston. She had appeared in a succession of gorgeous designer dresses for each evening's banquet.

Indulging in the historic splendour of the castle, Guy and Madonna took long walks around the 7,500-acre grounds. Guy reportedly went hunting, while Madonna joined in a clay-pigeon shoot and watched displays of falconry with best friends Gwyneth, Stella and Trudie.

"Scotland is dripping in atmosphere," Madonna swooned in an interview three months later. "It is so beautiful... You know ultimately, I'm a romantic. And my husband and I are both obsessed with history, and we wanted to go to a place that had history. He has really helped me appreciate the rawness and the roughness of nature. You can't really get away from it when you go up that far north in Scotland. Really, our choice was the result of a combination of things. His family is Scottish, on his father's side of the family, so he got to wear his family kilt, which was nice...

It was truly a magical, religious experience – the whole week."

Certainly, Madonna did seem visibly uplifted by the romantic traditions of Scotland – and by the upper-class lifestyle that her husband, Guy, had ironically tried to obscure in his own background as he became surrounded by a mystique involving East End wideboys and gangsters.

During this period, Madonna was photographed more than once wearing a tartan coat over her embroidered jeans, which may have set off a copycat reaction: within months, the likes of Courtney Love were snapped in tartan skirts. Madonna also embraced the trappings of the wealthy country set, appearing in tweed, Barbours, Hunter wellies and Holland & Holland jackets and travelling by Range Rover.

The Queen of Pop declared her admiration for the Queen of England, hobnobbed with Prince Charles – "a naughty little boy" – over dinner, and showed a growing interest in the aristocracy and in acquiring real class as opposed to nouveau-riche ostentation.

However, she has since had little opportunity to develop her aristocratic aspirations, moving as work has dictated between the family's homes – a Spanish-style hacienda in Beverly Hills and a listed, Georgian townhouse near London's Oxford Street. They recently had both houses refurbished.

Looking every inch the aristocrat, down to the simple jewellery and regal wave, Madonna emerges from Dornoch cathedral in December 2000 after the christening of baby Rocco (opposite). Madonna arrived in Scotland dressed in tweeds (below) to the strains of 'Like A Virgin' played on the bagpipes.

Who's That Girl?

Madonna was voted the most inspirational woman in the world in a 2001 survey. Voters in the *Celebrity Bodies* magazine poll believed she enjoyed the most enviable lifestyle, and they were specially impressed with her attitude, talent, career – and bank account. They also found she was the over-forty who had aged the best.

Magazine editor Alison Hall commented: "Madonna might be nudging middle age and she's not the most beautiful A-lister, but she's got the qualities we all deeply envy – endless talent, confidence and originality, and is a true superstar with lasting appeal."

Madonna has stated on many occasions that she organises and carries out her daily commitments with military precision, and sleeps only a few hours a night. She watches little television other than basketball, boxing and movies, listens to classical music, plays chess, collects antiques and focuses on family, culture and relaxation when she has time off from the varied demands of her working life. Her latest hobby is believed to be horse-riding.

Food

Madonna admits that she doesn't have "the cooking gene". But if she's not eating out or dining at friends' homes, she's likely to have her own cook on duty. In emergencies she can hire a chef for up to £1,000 a day.

She has observed a variety of strict dietary regimes especially while on tour. She tries to eat healthy, vegetarian foods with lots of salads in the face of her appetite for bad things like cheese and real butter and she is known to have a sweet tooth, with a liking for fudge and white chocolate.

On the "Drowned World" tour, she was said to be following a high-protein, low-fat, low-carbohydrate menu – in line with the diet recommended by her Ayurveda specialists.

At New York's Madison Square Garden, her backstage table reportedly offered zucchini flower amaretti, marjoram risotto croquettes, tofu crostini, Italian-style sashimi, king prawn ceviche, duck salami, rice cake, saffron conchiglione and chicken meatballs wrapped in shiso leaves.

This caused shrieks of horror from food experts who branded the selection "pretentious and artificial." One writer groaned: "She's got more protein on there than most people eat in a month."

In one of her favourite New York restaurants, Nobu, which has branches across the world, Madonna is supposedly partial to Toro Tartar- the fancy name for raw tuna with caviar – and green tea ice cream.

In her taste for Japanese food, Madonna is also opting for health. During macrobiotic diets, she has to cut out the dairy produce and sweet temptations that she adores, and feasts instead on grains, nuts, pulses and pasta, fish, fruit, seeds and soya foods.

But in pregnancy, she sometimes indulged in cravings: poached eggs, pizza, French fries, crisps, olives and butternut squash.

At various times, Madonna has stated that she likes popcorn, Rice Krispies and fish'n'chips.

Lately, she's become a great deal more flexible about what she eats, telling *Heat* magazine in the summer of 2001: "If you stop worrying about being fat you will not be fat, I swear to God. I'm telling you. I eat whatever I want."

She doesn't drink much alcohol as a rule, but rolls out the barrel with a couple of Martinis, a flute of champagne or the odd half of Guinness. Her backstage requirements during the "Drowned World" tour apparently comprised Red Bull and Starbucks cappuccino.

If she ever does overdo it, she cures a hangover with "a good workout to really loud music".

Going Out

When in London, Madonna has been known to lift a glass at the Sanderson and Claridges hotels, and in a variety of pubs including the Windsor Castle in Notting Hill and the Scarsgill Tavern in Kensington.

Restaurants she has been spotted in include San Lorenzo in Beauchamp Place, The Pharmacy in Notting Hill, Kensington Place in Kensington Church Street, Circus in Piccadilly, Blakes in Earl's Court, The Ivy in Covent Garden and Drones in Pont St, London SW1.

She has made club appearances in China White at Piccadilly, Kabaret off Regent Street and the Red Cube in Leicester Place.

Shopping expeditions have taken her to Koh Sumi in Covent Garden, Voyage in the Fulham Road, Harvey Nicks in Knightsbridge and Solange Azagury Partridge's jewellery shop in Westbourne Grove.

Reading and Writing

A firm believer in the art of letter-writing, Madonna conducted the early part of her courtship with Guy Ritchie by post. She told one interviewer: "You have to be able to write before you can come into my room. I mean, write me a good letter or fuck off."

She reads avidly, and lists among her favourite books *The Alchemist* by Paulo Coelho, *Captain Corelli's Mandolin* by Louis De Bernieres, *The Little Prince* by Antoine de Saint-Exupery, *Little Women* by Louisa May Alcott and *Memoirs Of A Geisha* by Arthur Golden, which inspired her recent Japanese look. She said: "Sometimes I think that what I do is like being a modern-day Geisha."

Her favourite writers cross the generations, the globe and stylistic boundaries. They include James Joyce, Jack Kerouac, JD Salinger, Sylvia Plath, Lawrence Durrell, Raymond Carver, F Scott Fitzgerald, Charles Bukowski, Alice Walker, Ernest Hemingway, Henry Walke, Kurt Vonnegut Jr, Francoise Sagen, Honore De Balzac, VS Naipaul, Henry James, Louise Edrich, Guy De Montpassant, Noel Coward, Pablo Neruda, Anne Sexton and 13th Century poet Jalaludin Rumi, whose writing is enjoying a renaissance.

Jellybean Benitez once remarked: "Many people don't realise how incredibly intelligent Madonna is. She loves English literature – Shakespeare, Keats and Dryden – and used to spend hours ploughing through their works... "

Yoga and Spirituality

Madonna gave up her strenuous training routines when pregnant with Lourdes and has become "gym-free... liberated!" She now commits an hour and a half a day, five days a week, to Ashtanga yoga, even if she has to get up at 6am to squeeze it in. Described as "kick-ass yoga", it's a vigorous, aerobic type of exercise which involves prayer chanting and continuous movement that builds lean, powerful muscles rather than the hard, tight bulk resulting from weight-lifting and conventional gym work.

She has said: "It taught me patience and judgement. It also taught me that you have to earn things, that just because you want to conquer something doesn't mean you're going to. Now I feel that yoga is a total metaphor for life."

In 2001, Madonna booked into an isolated, log-cabin retreat by a Colorado mountainside, complete with hot springs, open fires, antiques and a dedicated yoga cave.

This form of yoga can bring accompaniments such as Eastern-influenced clothing, Indian prayer beads and body art including mendhi henna tattoos, all of which Madonna has worn.

However, she did manage to upset a group of "sincere Hindus, Vaishnavas and yoga practitioners around the globe" when she appeared at the MTV Video Music Awards of 1998 wearing sacred facial markings while also revealing her nipples through a see-through top and moving in a "sexually suggestive manner". She retorted that "the essence of purity and divinity is non-judgement."

She's also said to have studied Kundalini yoga, involving meditation, chanting and deep breathing, and the fashionable, gentle exercise regime, Pilates.

Working in conjunction with yoga in Madonna's spiritual quest are Eastern philosophies, including Buddhism and Hinduism, the ancient Judaic mysticism of the Kabbalah, which teaches the relationship between the person and the universe, God, life and death, and significant elements of Catholicism that she has held through her struggles with the faith. She has treasured some of her favourite crucifixes and rosary beads, including a string of turquoise ones given to her by her grandmother which she regarded as "offbeat and interesting" when she tried it on.

Of her previous obsession with the crucifix, she said in *Time* magazine: "It's a beautiful kind of symbolism, the idea of someone suffering, which is what Jesus Christ on a crucifix stands for, and then not taking it seriously at all. Seeing it as an icon with no religiousness attached to it. It isn't a sacrilegious thing for me. I'm not saying, 'This is Jesus Christ and I'm laughing.'"

Meanwhile, Madonna has won a final battle with her old adversaries, the nuns. According to press reports, she demanded, and won, the website address of madonna.com, claiming that her worldwide fame gave her more right to the name of Madonna than the sisters at the Madonna Rehabilitation Hospital in Lincoln, Nebraska.

Health

It's reported that Madonna has also become an exponent of the old Indian science, Ayurveda, wherein each participant is identified as one of three personality types and advised on an appropriate diet and herbal and essential oils to de-stress and revitalise the body. With meditation and relaxation also included, the aim is to get the mind and body working holistically together.

Madonna allegedly practises this in conjunction with a hip, new, health technique called Biological Terrain Analysis, pioneered by Dr Laz Bannock. The procedure, like Ayurveda, is more about prevention than cure and is based on the idea of making the body healthy and harmonious.

Various fluids are analysed to discover possible areas of weakness, and diet and lifestyle changes are then recommended.

She is also said to have consulted with north London's "Barefoot Doctor" Stephen Russell whose treatments include acupuncture, hands-on healing, massage, hypnotherapy, martial arts, music therapy and Taoism.

However, Madonna's just like every other woman when she gets a headache. Her backstage essentials include a box of Advil painkillers.

Therapy

"It's all about self-examination and I don't just get it from therapy. I get it from a lot of different scenarios. I get it from my yoga teacher, when I look into my daughter's eyes. There are a lot of situations that are teaching."

Art

Madonna is a private art collector – and hangs the works on her walls at home. According to one visitor, there are paintings of naked ladies all over her 1926 Spanish hacienda home near Sunset Boulevard.

She famously adores the work of Mexican artist Frida Kahlo, the polio and accident victim and feminist heroine who died in 1954. Madonna's favourite Kahlo is the rather bloody "My Birth", which she owns, maintaining that anyone who dislikes the painting could never be her friend. She recently loaned another Kahlo, "Self-Portrait With Monkey", to a surreal art exhibition, "Desire Unbound", at London's Tate Modern gallery.

Madonna told *Grammy* magazine: "I worship her paintings because they speak of her sadness and her pain, but they are so beautiful and I relate to that in one's work. It's just that it took me a while to figure out how to translate the sad stuff into a song." She added, to *The Observer*: "I'm really interested in two things in art. One is suffering and the other is irony and a certain bizarre sense of humour."

She admires Fernand Leger – one of whose paintings hangs on her kitchen wall. "I kinda like that," said Madonna. "It's like having a fur coat that's too long and drags on the ground."

Other favourites are Tamara de Lempicka, Georgia O'Keeffe, Diego Rivera, Tina Modotti, Peggy Guggenheim, Edward Weston, Edward Hopper, William-Adolphe Bouguereau and Frenchman Gerard Priault. Dali and Picasso are among the "superstars" represented in her collection.

Madonna also follows the work of contemporary photographers such as Guy Bourdin, Nan Goldin, Inez Van Lamsweerde, Sean Ellis, Mario Sorrenti, Steven Meisel, Patrick Demarchellier, Mario Testino, Herb Ritts, Helmut Newton and Paolo Reversi.

However, Madonna still has a soft spot for "that whole downtown art scene" which brought influence to bear on her early career and acknowledges Andy Warhol, Keith Haring and Jean-Michel Basquiat.

Art, cinema and travel to places like Spain and North Africa – these are the things that Madonna says gave her a "real education". She said: "But you have to be attracted to them in the first place. Then your tastes get honed over time."

She added: "A lot of the art that I have has influenced me, and a lot of movies have inspired me."

"there's nothing remotely cool or cutting-edge about me right now"

Looking decidedly cool for a 42-year-old, Madonna continues to favour the jeans, chain and pseudo-punk T-shirt image when out and about (above), though her ultra fashion-conscious pale blue Prada ensemble is more striking.

Having described herself self-deprecatingly as a "domesticated cow", proclaiming that "there's nothing remotely cool or cutting-edge about me right now", Madonna, on the contrary, was entering into a productive and successful year 2001.

True, she was spending time at children's playgroups and Disneyland, and her new-found inclination to walk around the streets of her neighbourhood like any normal mum meant that she wasn't always prepared for the flash of cameras. Some unflattering pictures did appear in the gossip columns from time to time: Madonna in LA with sorry-looking hair, no make-up and a pair of jogging pants; Madonna in London, tearful and puffy-eyed in the back of a car with Guy; Madonna leaving a London party, tired and emotional. Mostly, though, she looked as striking as ever, even dressed down in casual pants and top to walk with Lourdes.

Cool in her stylish Chloe separates, head-turning in her blue, silk Prada top-and-breeches set complete with mandarin collar, on top of the trends in her limited-edition, Adidas 83-C tracksuit top and raunchy in her skintight leather jacket, scarf and jeans, Madonna still kept the photographers busy.

Appearing in a series of glossy magazine spreads in the first months of the year, Madonna, in her forties, looked glamorous, alluring. Paying tribute to Debbie Harry and Catherine Deneuve in *InStyle*, she perfected the cat's-eye look with thick lashes and some strategically drawn sweeps of liner under her eyes, and she modelled a punkish collection of silk, patent leather and chiffon clothes, largely black, worn with ties, fishnets, gloves and high-heeled boots. For *Elle*, the outfits were bold, fringed, flesh-baring and just plain fun.

Still she was setting trends. "Bobs are back!" blared one headline, in response to Madonna's straight, long and layered blonde cut. Other articles marvelled at her youthfulness, talked endlessly of the flattering beige and pink tones of her make-up, and analyzed her beauty secrets.

The high streets and catwalks exploded with Madonnamania in the early part of 2001. Lacy fashions recalling the 'Like A Virgin' era arrived in the department stores at knockdown prices, as did the crop-tops, studded cuffs and belts, rubber bangles and jingling bracelets of her breakthrough, trashy image.

Christian Dior recreated the famous jumble of clashing colours, bustiers, fishnets, mini-skirts and dangling crucifixes, while Moschino and Dolce & Gabbana drew inspiration from the more recent rhinestone cowgirl imagery, with all its denim and pink, stetson hats – a high street favourite. D&G also produced diamond-studded T-shirts bearing photographs of Madonna's album covers. The customised T-shirts, of course, were everywhere.

Perhaps the most bizarre tribute came from one of a

"This is an angry song and I wanted a matching visual"

group of charity fund-raisers who shook hands with Prince Charles in September wearing a dangerous-looking, conical bra that was worthy of the old Madonna herself.

With all of this excitement going on, Madonna proved in April that she hadn't lost her touch as an exciting video artist: she got censored again, this time in collaboration with her husband, perhaps inspired by the success of the acceptance skit they filmed for The Brits.

For the first time, Guy Ritchie directed a Madonna video – for 'What It Feels Like For A Girl', released in April 2001. In scenes that are occasionally hair-raising but filled with humour, an extremely feminine-looking Madonna with a short blonde bob, lots of eye make-up and cherry-tinted lipstick tucks herself into a boilersuit to take on the persona of a macho

male on a wrecking spree.

Screeching around the streets, her gran in tow, in a stolen, yellow Chevrolet with number plates reading PUSSY and CAT, she slams into other vehicles, knocks a young boy over, and carries out various opportunist crimes with a water pistol and a stungun. The smash scene at the end, in which she wraps a second stolen car around a pole, was considered too violent for regular viewing by both MTV and VH1. Both chose to show it only late at night, and then only occasionally.

"This is an angry song and I wanted a matching visual with an edgy dance mix," stated Madonna, adding that she hoped it would "make people ask questions and open dialogues".

Undeterred, the husband-and-wife team almost

The video for 'What It Feels Like For A Girl' was directed by Guy Ritchie and ran into trouble with the censors for its depiction of speeding and violence. As ever, Madonna commented that the video was designed to provoke, though violence is something Madonna has previously refused to glamourise. The Ritchie influence?

The Drowned World tour opened in Barcelona in June 2001, and Madonna was keen to show off her new guitar skills in 'Candy Perfume Girl'. For the show's European opening section, Madonna dressed in Gaultier's tartan punk outfit though the colour scheme was changed to black-and-white for the USA dates.

DROWNE

DROWNE

D WORLD

As with Madonna's previous outings, the Drowned World tour was an inherently theatrical production, with five different sections and elaborate dance routines. Most impressive was the *Crouching Tiger Hidden Dragon*-style routine for 'Sky Fits Heaven', while 'Human Nature' saw the diva ride a mechanical bull.

"It's all about theatre and drama and surprise and suspense"

For 'Holiday', Madonna donned a fur coat, velvet fedora and customised T-shirt (below), though first impressions of the message were soon changed when Madonna dropped the coat. Although the star has reputedly dropped the strenuous work-outs of earlier days, she still looks decidedly toned (opposite) for a 42-year-old mother of two.

immediately returned to action to film an ad for BMW in another high-speed drama with Madonna, trying to flee the paparazzi, being taken on a scary ride by actor Clive Owen.

Having scored her twenty-fourth gold disc in America with 'What It Feels Like For A Girl', putting her on an even footing with The Beatles, Madonna set off on the six-month "Drowned World" tour in June to promote the melodic electronica of *Music*.

The tour, which opened in Barcelona and arrived in the UK in July, found Madonna reviving some of her previous styles with a spectacular twist – and, for the first time, playing guitars onstage, having taken lessons especially, with the words "Fuck off" printed on her strap.

Sold-out, celebrity-packed audiences at her six-night residency at London's Earl's Court saw Madonna enter through billows of dry ice to open up with 'Drowned World'/'Substitute For Love' in authentic Kings Road/Gaultier punk garb – a sleeveless black, crossover top with one net sleeve, a tartan kilt, black trousers with zips and bondage straps, and a studded dog collar and wristband. Finishing the "punk" set with 'Beautiful Stranger' and 'Ray Of Light', she reappeared on a riser in an extraordinary, hand-painted, Gaultier geisha costume with Arianne Phillips' fifty-two-feet sleevespan, which was stretched to dramatic effect across the stage.

The thrills and spills came thick and fast, Big Top-style, as Madonna flew into the air to perform some breath-taking acrobatics with her team of ten dancers against a backdrop of trees and red sky, and was then transformed into a Ninja superwoman kickboxing and Samurai sword-fighting, suspended by wires and of course emerging victorious with a shotgun aloft – all with a nod to *Crouching Tiger, Hidden Dragon*.

The bedenimed, rhinestone cowgirl Madonna in a stars and stripes vest rode a mechanical bull during 'Human Nature', dressed largely by the Caten twins, line-danced around bales of hay, and performed flamenco moves during 'La Isla Bonita', her shoulder-length blonde hair scraped back as she showed off a glamorous, revealing, black, senorita's dress and trousers. Determinedly Latin, she sang a Spanish version of 'What It Feels Like For A Girl', in a section featuring altier style.

Closing the show with 'Holiday' and 'Music', she sported a ghetto-girl get-up, with a fake-fur coat, a fedora, black leather pants and the regulation black D&G T-shirt with its silver, sparkling letters spelling "Mother" at the front and "F*cker" at the back.

Madonna, characteristically, had wanted everything to be "absolutely perfect", but a gremlin or two did manage to get into the works. One night, her black, geisha wig slipped off her head, leaving the embarrassed star with a face like thunder. And on another night, a drunken fan staggered past security and on to the stage within inches of Madonna.

Some critics complained that the performance was short on classic songs such as 'Like A Prayer', while concentrating too heavily on material from *Ray Of Light* and *Music*. That, however, had been Madonna's intention. Once again, the show had been conceived more as a musical than a traditional concert, and its choreography and visuals were often awe-inspiring.

Before the tour began, Madonna had promised: "I don't see the point of doing a show unless you offer something that is going to mind-boggle the senses. It's not enough to get onstage and sing a song. It's all about theatre and drama and surprise and suspense."

As usual, she was as good as her word.

Taking Care Of Business

Madonna set up her record label, Maverick, in April 1992 with $60 million from Warner Bros and a clear idea of how she was going to do things: "My goal, of course, is to have hits with the new company," she said. "I'm not one of these dumb artists who is just given a label to shut her up. I asked for a record company. So I'm not going to be invisible or simply phone in my partnership. There's no honour or satisfaction in palming the work off to someone else."

Madonna's partner was her friend Guy Oseary, who took charge of A&R responsibilities, and the President was her manager, Freddie DeMann. Oseary was reportedly an ex-boyfriend of one of DeMann's daughters.

Madonna involved herself in all aspects of the organization and made a speciality of diplomacy, bringing a human touch to Maverick's dealings with the artists they wanted to sign.

However, there were times when Madonna's famous charm was not enough. Rumours abounded that her first three proposed signings – Courtney Love's band Hole, Rage Against The Machine and Presidents Of The USA – all turned down the Maverick opportunity.

In 1993, the multi-million-selling Candlebox, an alternative rock band, scored the label's first hit, and there was great critical acclaim and six Grammy nominations for black singer Me'shell Ndegeocello. But it was with Alanis Morissette that Maverick became a major force, selling thirty million copies worldwide of her *Jagged Little Pill* album.

Morissette said of her initial dealings with Madonna: "We had a couple of girlie nights. We are so intense, we always seem to end up really talking. We're so alike in a lot of ways. We don't have the same taste in men, but we have the same philosophies about dynamics with men... "

There were no such cosy evenings with the Prodigy. They were being chased for a licensing deal by lots of American labels, but they chose Maverick because they liked Oseary and DeMann who were laid-back but eager and straightforward.

Madonna, typically, turned up for the meetings, impressing the band's UK label representatives with her unusual but relevant lines of questioning.

So what was in it for Madonna? By all accounts, seven albums with an advance of five million dollars on each, to be released through Maverick Entertainment. She was also financially responsible to Warners, who could recoup their investment against her royalties.

The original plan was for Maverick to be a multi-media company, but after a couple of disappointing ventures into film with *Dangerous Game* and *Canadian Bacon*, it was decided to stick to music.

There have been hiccups along the way. In 1997, DeMann stepped down as Madonna's manager and became Chief Executive of Maverick. The next year, he left the label too, after some legal squabbling. Rumour has it that Madonna gave him a generous handshake as he left the building.

By then, she had recruited Caresse Norman as her personal manager, and hired the powerful management team of Peter Mensch and Chris Bernstein.

By 2001, Maverick was reported to be in some difficulty, with its star artist Alanis Morissette having failed to match the phenomenal sales of *Jagged Little Pill*. Indeed, Madonna's spokeswoman, Liz Rosenberg, admitted that there had been "some issues regarding Alanis and her relationship with Maverick", but they were said to have been resolved amicably. The Prodigy, meanwhile, had taken an extended break from musical activity.

Madonna, idealistically, had been interested in signing artists of artistic value, but credibility doesn't always equal sales, and many of her talented brood simply never caught on.

In July, it was splashed in newspapers around the world that Madonna had authorised a shake-up in which six executives had left the company. They included President Bill Bennett. Maverick's Ronnie Dashev told the *New York Post*: "Madonna's involved in all the major decisions at the company."

Maverick mavericks (far left page clockwise from top) Candlebox, No Authority, Muse, Erasure. (This page clockwise from top left) Prodigy, Michelle Branch, Deftones, Insolence, Madonna with Cleopatra.

Reuters reported that Maverick's second-quarter revenues had fallen by eleven per cent to $895 million and that cash-flow had plunged by thirty-three per cent to $87 million. In view of this, rumours of a new Madonna compilation set may not seem outlandish.

Maverick was not Madonna's first venture into business. Determined to control every aspect of her career, and known to work long hours on her financial affairs, she had already launched her clothing line, Wazoo; Boy Toy, Inc., a company dealing with her music and record royalties; Slutco, a video production company that she wound up and replaced with Siren Films, concerned with movie and video production; Webo Girl for music publishing; and Music Tours, Inc. for live work.

By the autumn of 2001, the Maverick roster brought together Alanis Morissette, Amanda Baxter, Binocular, Candlebox, Cleopatra, Dalvin Degrate, Deftones, Ebba Forsberg, Erasure, Insolence, Jude, Love Spit Love, Madonna, Me'shell Ndegeocello, Mest, Michelle Branch, Muse, Neurotic Outsiders, No Authority, Olive, Onesidezero, Prodigy, The Rentals, Showoff, Solar Twins, Summercamp, Swimmer, Tantric, Unloco and William Orbit.